KU-541-923

BW

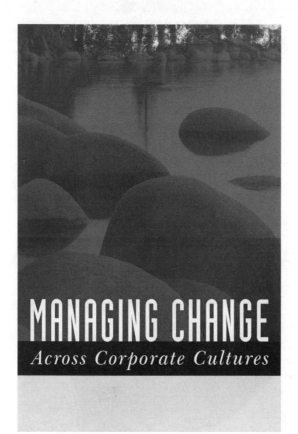

MANAGING CHANGE

Across Corporate Cultures

SOMERSET COLLEGES

Y06246

For our partners Pek Lan and Cens,
whose patience seems to be unlimited.

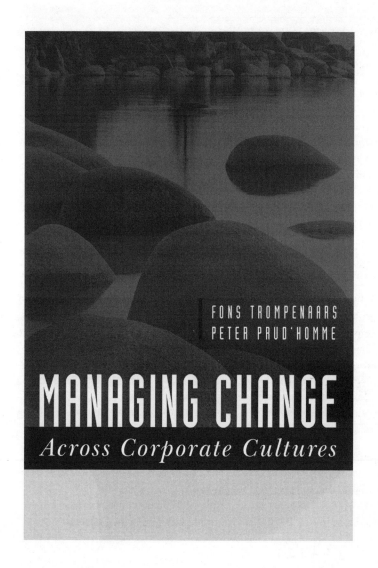

FONS TROMPENAARS
PETER PRUD'HOMME

MANAGING CHANGE

Across Corporate Cultures

YEOVIL COLLEGE
LIBRARY

CAPSTONE

Copyright © 2004 by Fons Trompenaars and Peter Prud'homme van Reine

The right of Fons Trompenaars and Peter Prud'homme van Reine to be
identified as the authors of this work has been asserted in accordance with the
Copyright, Designs and Patents Act 1988

First published 2004 by
Capstone Publishing Ltd (a Wiley Company)
The Atrium
Southern Gate
Chichester
West Sussex PO19 8SQ
England
www.wileyeurope.com

All rights reserved. Except for the quotation of short passages for the
purposes of criticism and review, no part of this publication may be
reproduced, stored in a retrieval system, or transmitted, in any form or by any
means, electronic, mechanical, photocopying, recording or otherwise, without
the prior permission of the publisher. Requests to the publisher should be
addressed to the Permissions Department, John Wiley & Sons Ltd, The
Atrium, Southern Gate, Chichester, West Sussex PO19 8SQ, England, or
emailed to permreq@wiley.co.uk, or faxed to (+44) 1243 770571.

CIP catalogue records for this book are available from the British Library and
the US Library of Congress

ISBN 1-84112-578-4

Typeset by Forewords, 109 Oxford Road, Cowley, Oxford

Printed and bound by T.J. International Ltd, Padstow, Cornwall

10 9 8 7 6 5 4 3 2 1

This book is printed on acid-free paper responsibly manufactured from
sustainable forestry in which at least two trees are planted for each one used
for paper production.

Substantial discounts on bulk quantities of Capstone Books are available to
corporations, professional associations and other organizations. For details
contact John Wiley & Sons: tel. (+44) 1243 770441, fax (+44) 1243 770517,
email corporatedevelopment@wiley.co.uk

Contents

Acknowledgements

In preparing this book, we have been significantly assisted by the many companies with which we have worked and the managers who provided us with many case examples. Thanks are also due to Maaike Tjallingii for additional research, Professor Peter Woolliams for support with graphics, and Charles Hampden-Turner for continuous inspiration. Last but not least, we could not have completed the task without the support of our families.

INTRODUCTION

Only one in five change programs deliver the benefits expected of them. Such was the assessment of A.T. Kearney, stated in *The Economist* in 2000, and we can well believe it. All too often, temporary improvement is not sustained. Many initiatives have achieved some short-term cost reductions while real change has proven elusive.

In our view, the high failure rate of change initiatives is due to the fact that "change leaders," "change agents," and "change consultants" are struggling with the role of corporate culture in change processes.

For many, corporate culture (or organizational culture) is still an elusive concept. It has been variously defined as a system of publicly and collectively accepted "meanings" which operate for a group at a particular time (Trice and Beyer, 1984); a pattern of "basic assumptions" developed as the group or organization learns to cope with its environment (Schein, 1985), and more simply as "the way we do things around here" (Deal and Kennedy, 1982). Yet despite the numerous strategic and culture change programs that have been initiated by organizations in recent years, efforts directed at identifying specific, observable, and therefore measurable features of corporate culture have met with far less success.

Throughout the extensive literature on change management per se, many authors have attempted to identify and categorize approaches to change, some from human systems perspectives, some from organization theory, and some from a general systems view. Many such summaries appear to have ignored earlier categorical and analytical frameworks for change. Let's look briefly at the work of Chin and Benne from 1969 and that of Sashkin and Egermeier from 1992:

Evolving approaches to change

Chin and Benne (1969)	Sashkin and Egermeier (1992)
Empirical–rational	Fix the parts
Power–coercive	Fix the people
Normative–reeducative	Fix the organization

The basic assumption underlying the empirical–rational model is that individuals are rational and will follow their rational self-interest. Thus if a "good" change is suggested, well-intentioned people will adopt it.

The power–coercive approach relies on influencing individuals and systems to change through legislation and external leverage where power of various types is the dominant factor. Power–coercive strategies emphasize political, economic, and moral sanctions, with the focus on using power of some type to "force" individuals to adopt the change concerned. One strategy is nonviolent protest and demonstrations. A second strategy is the use of political institutions to achieve change – for example, changing educational policies through state-level legislation. In the normative–reeducative approach, individuals are seen as being actively in search of satisfying needs and interests. Individuals do not passively accept what comes, but take action to advance their goals. Furthermore, changes are not only rational responses to new information but occur at the more personal level of values and habits. In addition, individuals are guided by social and institutional norms. The overarching principle of this model is that individuals must take part in their own change (reeducation) if it is to occur.

Sashkin and Egermeier conclude that, in a fix-the-parts approach, the "more personal assistance and continuing support from a skilled and knowledgeable local agent, the more likely that the innovation will be used for a long duration." In the fix-the-people approach the focus is on improving the knowledge and skills of employees, thus enabling them to perform their roles. Fixing the organization addresses the transition from a current corporate culture to an ideal corporate culture. It is to be noted that Sashkin and Egermeier themselves conclude that none of the three approaches has achieved long-term success, as shown in their studies…

Prescriptions for different approaches to change are often ethno-centric and may only be appropriate in the cultures where they were researched, developed, and validated. Whilst Harrison (1999) claims a methodology led by HR and based on early involvement to overcome assumed resistance, it may work in his stereotypical (national) culture, but is unlikely to be generally applicable to different industries – let alone different countries. Similiary, Abraham *et al.* (1997) report a successful methodology based on maintaining concern for quality – but again based on a stereotypical (corporate) role culture organization.

It appears more difficult to delineate and explain business failures that owe their origin to badly managed change initiatives. Bennett (1998) has observed that two most common explanations for the failure of change programmes derived from a lack of senior management commitment and a failure to address the "softer" issues related to reengineering's impact on people and corporate cultures. His view is that there is a more fundamental reason for many failed change transformation efforts, in particular that the basic vision that guides many change experts is flawed. Their "unconstrained vision," or view that mankind is infinitely perfectible, drives their change initiatives to solutions that break down in implementation, either because these solutions cannot cope with the complexities of the real world or because they encounter overwhelming organizational resistance. Even gurus, who have studied change manage ment and published their findings and frameworks extensively, have failed when they tried to apply their theories to their own situations. For example, Covey may have sold 13 million copies of his *7 Habits of Highly Effective People,* but he has been unsuccessful in his attempt to create a juggernaut of efficiency training (Business Week, 1999).

Based on the many models and analyses in the existing literature, together with our own evidence at Trompenaars Hampden-Turner, derived from extensive, worldwide research and consulting, we can begin to draw several conclusions:

1. Change may be planned or unplanned, evolutionary or revolutionary.

2. Most change will continue to be brought about by influences in the corporation's external environment.

3. In order to survive and prosper, organizations must change and adapt – as least as fast as their environment is changing.

4. Change itself is inevitable – and the real issue becomes change management.

5. Change management processes are critical to organizational success because they act as agents which influence every other organizational process.

6. Badly managed change can result in:
    negative organizational memory about change and how change is managed
    a retarded ability to undertake any change programs in the future
    negative impacts on organizational performance and morale

negative bottom-line impact

accelerated onset of crises.

7.   Existing approaches to managing change may be summarised as:

change of executive leadership

change in mid-management leadership roles

management development programs

survey/feedback programs

quality circles/TQM

business process reengineering (BPR).

8.   While the world and organizations are changing, many fundamental assumptions about any one industry, competitors,
people, and technology tend to go unnoticed and unchallenged.

In preparing our organizations for the twenty-first century, new
change management processes must provide a mechanism for sur-
facing and rethinking our deeply held assumptions. Otherwise
meaningful change is not possible.

We believe it is all too simple, as happens in many traditional change
approaches, to begin to address these factors as "what," "why,"
and/or "how" questions. Let's look at the problems these pose.

Change as a "how" problem

To frame the change effort in the form of "how" questions is to focus
the effort on means. Diagnosis is assumed or not performed at all.
Consequently, the ends sought are not discussed.

Change as a "what" problem

To focus on ends requires the posing of "what" questions. What are we trying to accomplish? What changes are necessary? What indicators will signal success? What standards apply? What measures of performance are we trying to affect? Ends and means are relative notions, not absolutes; that is, something is an end or a means only in relation to something else. Thus chains and networks of ends–means relationships often have to be traced before one finds the "real" end of a change effort.

Change as a "why" problem

The "why" question is claimed to be useful because it reveals the true end of a change effort. However, it leads to an oversimplified view of management's task of reducing resistance to change and increasing the forces for change.

In an environment full of contradictions, business leaders are constantly being torn between acting quickly and planning for the future, competing and cooperating, concentrating on core competencies and expanding into new markets, downsizing and taking care of employees, managing tasks and managing issues, taking risks and avoiding costly mistakes. To succeed in such an environment, managers need to develop a capacity for thriving on paradoxes. This involves adopting a mindset that is open to contradictions, cultivating paradoxes, and engaging paradoxes. Managing contradictions requires a new logic, for which we offer a new approach. By applying an inductive analysis to our evidence and research data, we offer a "through" question approach in this book:

Change as a "through" problem

How can we, *through* the current value or behavior that we want to keep, get more of the ideal value we want to strive for?

While cultures differ markedly in how they approach these paradoxes or dilemmas, they do not differ in needing to make some kind of response. They share the destiny of facing up to different challenges of existence. Once change leaders have become aware of the problem solving process that we offer here, they will become more successful by looking at corporate cultural change as a through–through process.

Fons adds:

This book takes the past very seriously. Once you know that an organization is essentially a social and cultural construct there is an increasing need to gain an insight into how corporate culture plays a role. For many years THT has focused on international differences. We have become increasingly aware that organizational culture plays a very important role, even in cases where the initial assumption is that national culture dominates.

Peter Prud'homme, my colleague and co-author, has dedicated the last few years to going beyond the cookie-cutter approach of corporate culture and has introduced nine basic "entry points" that are specific to organizational culture. This approach, related to the dimensions of national culture we developed at THT in the last decades, can reveal many more subtle organizational differences. Furthermore, in this book we try not to limit ourselves by capturing those differences through examples and instruments, but show how to reconcile those differences on higher levels.

This has led to our view of organizational culture as a "pattern by which a company connects different value orientations, such as rules versus exceptions, people focus versus focus on reaching goals and targets, decisiveness versus consensus, controlling the environment versus adapting to it, in such a way that they work together in a mutually enhancing way." Cultures can learn to reconcile such values at ever higher levels of attainment, for instance by creating better rules from the study of numerous exceptions. This corporate culture pattern shapes a shared identity which helps to make corporate life meaningful for the members of the organization, and contributes to their intrinsic motivation for doing its work. In this book we argue that the "Reconciling Organization," an organization with an inherent capacity to reconcile dilemmas by connecting different value orientations, will be significantly more successful and changeable than any organization that simply chooses to go for the extreme ends of the polar system.

Do note that, although this book is part of the Culture for Business series, it can be read separately from the others – *Business Across Cultures, Managing People Across Cultures* and *Marketing Across Cultures.* Readers may also find it useful – and interesting – to visit the website for the series: www.cultureforbusiness.com.

Enjoy!

Amsterdam, February 2004

CHAPTER 1

Understanding corporate culture

WHAT CORPORATE CULTURE REALLY IS

The story about the CEO of an American company who, in around 1985, said to consultants: "We need a corporate culture in this company too. Get me one in two weeks" is perhaps apocryphal. Even so, it became a symbol for the corporate culture hype created by influential publications at that time. The message of the story is not just that corporate cultures cannot be created in two weeks. The CEO in the story may not have been aware of it, but each established company already has a corporate culture – not one designed by managers and consultants but one rooted in the history and tradition of the company concerned, and in the values of all its people. It does more to hold the company together than its management may realize. Executives who neglect corporate culture or have a too-optimistic view about it should be prepared for a tough wake-up call, in the form of hard lessons with problems in mergers, acquisitions, and joint ventures: "We did not realize we had such a strong corporate culture, and that it would be so different from that of our new partner." There are equally hard lessons to be learned in failed change initiatives: "We did not expect that our current corporate culture would hinder us in making our change program successful."

Three things have not changed since the mid-1980s. Corporate culture is still critical to an organization's success or failure. It is still something you cannot acquire in two weeks. And there is still confusion about what corporate culture actually *is*.

Here are four of the numerous definitions of corporate culture:

• The way we do things around here.

- A system of informal, unwritten rules.
- A system of shared values, beliefs, assumptions that guide attitudes, behaviors, systems, and practices in our organization.
- What the members of the organization perceive as being central, enduring, and distinctive about it.

In fact, each of these definitions reveals a different layer of corporate culture.

Use of language

In the end corporate culture does show up in "how we do things around here." These are the things that can be seen or observed: the formal organizational structure, formal systems and processes, routines such as staff meetings, behaviors of the members of the organization such as the way people dress, symbols such as the size of offices, the titles on business cards, the type of lease cars that people are entitled to drive, and the way people use language, including any specialized terms or jargon used in their organization.

The last issue, language, is often underestimated. In verbal communication, is using foul language acceptable, as it is in many "tough guy" companies such as broking firms, or is it the end of your career? Do you address recipients of emails with their first name – just "Peter" – with "Dear Peter," or does it have to be Dear Mr/Mrs/Ms Jones or even Dear Dr Jones? Do you end the email with "best wishes," "thanks," or just "regards"? Each organization has its own standards for what it considers acceptable.

Corporate cultures can be assessed by analyzing verbal and non-verbal communication. One of the ways to assess a corporate culture is to analyze its annual reports and other official publications; words that pop up often will tell you something about that corporate culture. For example, managers in French organizations tend to use the word "responsible" frequently, which confirms the importance of organizational structures and hierarchy.

In addition, every organization uses acronyms which everyone inside understands, though outsiders won't have a clue to their meaning. "Lobs" used to be IBM jargon for "Lines of Business." "GAM" is consultancy-speak for a Global Account Manager. All organizations have their "famous words" – which are sometimes very visible, such as Sam Walton's "everyday low prices" which can be seen all over the place at Wal-Mart outlets. Nokia's "connecting people" and Philips' "let's make things better" were introduced explicitly as expressions of a new way of working.

"How we do things around here"

"How we do things around here" is a popular definition of corporate culture among those consultants who promise a quick fix. It suggests that changing a corporate culture is simply changing just that, altering the way things are done: flatten the organization structure, introduce a new reward system, draft a "code of conduct," specify acceptable and unacceptable behaviors, specify acceptable and unacceptable use of language, make some changes at the symbolic level such as allowing casual clothing on Fridays. Some companies have introduced a "corporate song" hoping this would help (as it supposedly did with Japanese companies) in changing to a more collective, team-oriented culture. At THT we keep a copy of a tape with the corporate song of a brewing company which has the chorus "We're making great beer and we're making friends." What often tells you more about the corporate culture is "how people do things around here when they're not being watched." In this particular case, unfortunately for the brewer, the words of the corporate song were twisted by some employees to "We're making great beer and we're making big money," which came closer to how they really thought and felt about their organization.

The informal, unwritten rules

Knowing "how we do things around here" is just the start of understanding a corporate culture. You have to dig deeper to understand how the formal structures, systems, processes, and routines really work, and to find out the meaning behind behaviors, symbols, and language: "The way things really are around here."

That is where corporate culture as a system of informal, unwritten rules comes in. Informal rules are what you learn as a newcomer in an organization during your socialization process. Knowing the informal rules helps in understanding how decisions are really made, who the real key opinion makers in the organization are, and what you will really be rewarded for. The staff meeting that may look like an open decision making forum to an outsider is suddenly different when you know the informal rule that there should be no surprises, and that you need to lobby with influential people before the meeting if you want support for a new idea. Old hands in your company may tell you, as a newcomer, that although hours are officially 8.30 a.m. to 5.00 p.m., the only thing that really counts is never going home earlier than your boss. Or they may tell you that having lunch in the company restaurant with the right people would do more for your career than the formal assessment system. These people will tell you the things to avoid doing at all costs because they would be the end of your career. So while managers are supposed to ask for feedback from subordinates, you may be told that challenging a senior executive's decision is not such a great idea, even if the decision is obviously stupid. The old hands can also tell you the things you can get away with, even although they are not in line with formal policies or codes of conduct. For instance, as we once found in a consultancy company, they may tell you that you can get away with canceling internal appointments if you can use an important client's request as an excuse.

Heroes

Informal rules are also to be found in the stories and jokes that people tell about the company and its heroes. One of the reasons why Dilbert cartoons are so popular is that copies stuck to surfaces around the workplace serve as implicit messages about actual company life. Corporate stories often contain such implicit messages to reinforce the corporate culture by reminding people of the history of the company, by demonstrating that organizational objectives are attainable, or by giving prescriptions for desired behavior. For instance, corporate stories often remind people of the leadership's expectations. In the European operation of a Japanese dairy food company, local staff frequently told the story of how the Japanese director helped to load the trucks when customer demand was unexpectedly high the first week after start up. Leaders were indeed expected to show flexibility and to demonstrate that they were teamworkers. The story of how Amazon's founder Jeff Bezos improvised desks from materials bought at Home Depot in his converted garage is well-known in the company, reinforcing the importance of frugality and flexibility. In sales organizations, stories about exceptional customer service are common. Southwest Airlines' former CEO Herb Kelleher is known as a great storyteller, but he is not the only one in that company. Southwest has a Culture Committee consisting of organizational storytellers from all over the business who act as ambassadors for its corporate culture. One of Southwest Airlines' stories is about the conversation between its founders Rollin

King and Herb Kelleher that marked the start of the company: "Herb, let's start an airline," "Rollin, you're crazy. Let's do it!" (Freiberg and Freiberg, 1996). Whether authentic or not, the story serves the purpose of reinforcing the informal rule of "let's do it" in Southwest's culture.

Finding out who the heroes are in a particular company is another way of finding out the informal rules of a corporate culture. At Dell the heroes are the people who save costs. In other companies they may be those with the most brilliant ideas, the best political connections, or, as in most consultancy companies, the ones who bring in the highest fees.

Shared values

To understand where the informal rules originate, we have to go to a deeper layer of culture. That is where culture as a system of shared values comes in. Values are guiding principles with intrinsic importance to those inside the company. Where rules and norms define what people think they should do, values refer to shared orientation of what they desire to do. Values guide attitudes, behaviors, systems, and practices but are more stable. Teamwork, conflict avoidance, respect for hierarchy, frugality, customer orientation, punctuality, personal responsibility, professionalism, open communication, minimizing risk, pragmatism are all examples of possible values. While systems, practices, and rules can be changed almost instantly, values cannot be altered just like that. Introducing a performance-based pay system and drafting lists of desired behaviors may change daily practices, but won't automatically change the underlying values. Telling people that their performance will be evaluated based on criteria such as "understanding and meeting customer needs" won't automatically instil customer orientation as a value. People will find a way to score highly on that criteria when you introduce such a system; they may well continue to follow informal rules that work contrary to customer orientation but are in line with existing values which are more deeply rooted, such as giving priority to requests from the boss. Simply adding "customer obsession" to a list of core values won't change things instantly, either.

The real shared values are not necessarily identical to such a list of "core values." You probably won't find a core value of "not killing clients," since that would be – hopefully – taken for granted. When a value becomes a norm it slips out of consciousness. Very often the main reason for companies defining and publishing their core values is because they know that their people don't believe in them. Professional services companies usually put "teamwork" on their lists, though their reward systems stimulate extremely individualistic behaviour. Japanese companies never list teamwork as a core value because they take it for granted. Organizations that have "respect" on their lists of core values are often the ones where disrespectful behaviour is the rule. Many core values, such as concern for people, innovation, quality, customer service, and social responsibility are in reality only desired or aspirational values. They reflect a desired new culture, not the existing corporate culture.

At THT we vividly remember a two-day workshop with a company in the food industry. The aim was to discuss its new core values with its top 35 managers. "Openness" was one of those new values, but all of the managers, except for the four board members, perceived many hindrances to "living" this value in this company, which had a tradition of secrecy and "only communicating what people really need to know." On the evening of the first day of this corporate core values workshop one of the board members approached us and said: "Don't you think that we've talked enough about openness?" We began to understand the worries of his next-level managers.

So there may be a difference between what top managers see as core values and what the rest of the company sees as central to the organization. There may also be differences in how a value is interpreted between other internal groups. In an advisory firm, customer service may be interpreted as "helping the customer to ensure compliance with regulatory requirements" by the accountants, while the consultants in the same firm may interpret the same value as "satisfying the customer so that we get more lucrative consultancy projects." This actually happened at Arthur Andersen, as we will discuss later.

What organization members perceive as central

Therefore corporate culture, defined as "what the organization members perceive as central, enduring, and distinctive about the organization" (and, as Ed Schein of MIT has added, how they think and feel about it) brings us closer to the core of what organizational culture is.

Values must be perceived as central and enduring before people will really believe in them. If they are only seen as empty words uttered by top management, they will never become unspoken assumptions. Over time, if assumptions seem to work, they acquire the status of truths and are taught to new members of the group as the correct way to perceive, think, and feel. We follow Schein (Schein, 1985) in calling this a "pattern of basic assumptions" as in his definition of corporate culture:

> A pattern of assumptions, invented, discovered, or developed by a given group, as it learns to cope with the problem of external adaptation and internal integration, that has worked

well enough to be considered valid, and be taught to new members, as the correct way to perceive, think, and feel in relation to these problems.

While values can be articulated with relative ease, basic assumptions are tacit and taken for granted. Just as "core values" are often aspirational and not identical to the current values of a company, basic assumptions are not necessarily the same as those written in corporate philosophies, or in purpose or mission statements. These may be aspirational as well and may not be a reflection of the actual basic assumptions of the people in the company. There are, however, companies in which aspirational corporate philosophies do match the tacit basic assumptions; for instance, companies where the influence of the founder(s) is still pervasive. The philosophy of Swedish furniture company IKEA – "We offer a wide range of home furnishing systems of good design and function, at prices so low that the majority of people can afford them" – was developed by its founder, Ingvar Kamprad (Torekull, 1998), and does reflect the basic assumptions of simplicity, frugality, and egalitarianism which are central and enduring for this company.

Some companies manage to preserve corporate philosophies over generations of leaders, while constantly renewing themselves. 3M's "15 percent rule", encouraging technical people to devote 15 percent of their time to projects of their own choosing, was inspired by one of 3M's great inventors in the 1940s (3M Company, 2002). Stories about how the 15 percent rule contributes to the company's success are repeated so often that it helps to reinforce 3M's basic assumption that innovation, taking on new challenges, and not being afraid of making mistakes are central to it. Establishing an innovator award for exemplary use of the 15 percent time is the visible symbol of this tacit assumption.

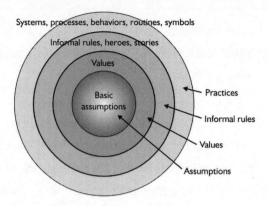

Figure 1.1 The layers of corporate culture

Figure 1.1 (after Schein) shows the different layers of corporate culture. At the surface are the formal structures, systems and processes, the routines, behaviors, and symbols. We can see and observe these, for instance in organization charts, in the formal decision making process, in the formal reward system, in the corporate image to the outer world ("corporate citizenship"), in how customers are served, in how people cooperate and work in teams, in how they communicate, in the working hours, in how people are dressed. In the next layer we discover the informal rules, for instance those dealing with status and authority, the informal decision-making process, the expectations of leadership and how people are motivated, the informal rules on how the company deals with its communities and environment. In the next layer are the values that guide those informal rules, behaviors, systems, and practices. At the core we find the basic assumptions, the tacitly-agreed correct way to perceive, think, and feel in relation to problems of internal integration and external adaptation.

These basic assumptions form a consistent and enduring, although not static, identity. This survives changes of leadership, economic downturns, technological breakthroughs, and new theories about what effective management is.

DILEMMAS OF CORPORATE CULTURE

By defining culture in terms of shared values and assumptions we do not want to suggest that companies have a single, static, identifiable culture and that strong, cult-like cultures are the ideal corporate culture model. Actually one should beware of cult-like cultures because they are not open for change in the environment and suppress internal divergence. Organizations have to survive in a complex, dynamic, and ambiguous environment. The opportunities and threats in the external environment lead to paradoxical demands: the need for internal control on the one hand and the need to adapt to the external environment on the other. The reality is, therefore, that corporate cultures need to be open for change and for diverse views themselves.

Corporate culture must facilitate spotting the opportunities and threats in the external environment and must also facilitate a dynamic response in adapting to it. Corporate culture must not suppress internal divergence, but must give an answer to the question of how to make use of diversity. Most companies have many different subcultures. One could distinguish between a top management culture, with financial issues high on the list of priorities, a middle management culture more occupied with day-to-day operational management, and a workforce culture where job security, wages, and working conditions having a high priority. Or one could distinguish between an engineering culture, dominated by technical specialists, and a commercial culture, dominated by sales and marketing people. In addition, each corporate division and each geographical region tend to have different cultures.

Many problems within organizations are caused by conflicts between the different value orientations related to these different cultures. Despite these conflicts, one can still talk about a corporate culture. Both these internal conflicts between different value orientations and the problems of external adaptation often come in the form of dilemmas. Corporate culture is what develops in the efforts to deal with these dilemmas. Organizational members continuously resolve dilemmas and these become basic assumptions when the solutions work. The art of creating a viable corporate culture is not to choose a fixed set of value orientations but to reconcile these contrasts or dilemmas.

In order for organizations to be effective, they need to pursue paradoxical criteria simultaneously and reconcile them. Here are three examples:

> On the one hand, corporate culture provides stability, focus, direction, and guidance: It establishes an internal way of life and sets patterns for internal relationships, it helps increase mutual understanding, trust, binds together people from different national cultures, defines effective and ineffective performance, and gives a framework for strategy and management approach. On the other hand, corporate culture needs to be capable of self-renewal and needs to reinvent itself continuously. In short, corporate culture needs to combine consistency and resilience.

> On the one hand, as a company we want an emphasis on developing our human resources; on the other hand, we want to focus on reaching goals and targets.

> On the one hand we need to take quick decisions even if there

are conflicting opinions, while on the other hand we need to build company-wide consensus to get everybody on board.

We then come to the following definition of corporate culture:

Corporate culture is the pattern by which a company connects different value orientations – such as rules versus exceptions, people focus versus focus on reaching goals and targets, decisiveness versus consensus, controlling the environment versus adapting to it – in such a way that they work together in a mutually enhancing way. Cultures can learn to reconcile such values at ever higher levels of attainment, for instance by creating better rules from the study of numerous exceptions. This corporate culture pattern shapes a shared identity which helps to make corporate life meaningful for the members of the organization, and contributes to their intrinsic motivation for doing the company's work.

THE RECONCILING CORPORATE CULTURE

We are going to use the term "reconciling corporate culture" in this book for a corporate culture with an inherent capacity to reconcile dilemmas by connecting different value orientations. This way of looking at corporate culture is very different from the traditional concept of "strong" corporate cultures, which describes corporate culture in terms of a set of value polarities dominating and militating against another polarity. That is a type of culture that says "you're either with us or you're against us". Such cultures can be successful in the short term within a certain context, but will be stressful and will also stagnate in the long term. Our definition of corporate culture is more dynamic. Instead it says: "We are 'against' you and critical of your behavior because you're a friend who needs help." Defining corporate culture in terms of how dilemmas are reconciled (or not) acknowledges that cultures are dynamic because reconciliation is a continuous process based on a dialogue between different value orientations.

Our definition of corporate culture also acknowledges that corporate cultures are inherently ambiguous and paradoxical. Corporate culture is not just the sum of more or less tangible cultural manifestations such as symbols, language, behaviors, stories, humor, rules, and values. How people interpret the cultural manifestations and how they are linked together is reflected in an underlying pattern of meaning, the pattern in which value differences are reconciled. We can then talk about corporate culture as shared networks of meaning, providing coherence and a sense of commitment even though the pattern of meaning is continuously reconstructed in an ongoing process of reconciliation. This way of looking at corporate culture acknowledges that a corporate culture needs to constantly reinvent itself, because the way people in the organization perceive, think, and feel in relation to problems of internal integration and external adaptation needs to change as well. Looking at corporate culture in terms of how it reconciles value differences helps managers in understanding the core of their company's culture and in changing day-to-day behaviors. This contrasts with a definition of corporate culture in terms of one fixed set of value polarities which will not resolve ambiguity, paradox, and conflict.

In the next part of this chapter we will look at the history of how the corporate culture concept has developed. We will see that, in an attempt to link corporate culture to success, corporate culture theory has focused on a static approach to corporate culture, and has thereby ignored this dynamic view.

CORPORATE CULTURE: A SUCCESS FACTOR OR A PROBLEM?

Corporate culture as a buzzword

An enormous interest in corporate culture was triggered in the 1980s by some influential publications in which it was presented as a success factor in business. This started in 1981 with Pascale and Athos's *The Art of Japanese Management*. Around 1980, Japan severely challenged Corporate America's dominance; the success of Japanese companies was attributed to their unique corporate culture. Pascale and Athos argued that there was a lot to learn from Japanese corporate cultures, especially in how they handled the soft aspects of management. In their book they focused on how corporate philosophies and values instilled harmony between management and workforce, on the leadership styles (such as concern for employees, including their social life) and human resource management practices (such as lifetime employment) that made it possible to tap the skills and knowledge of all employees, especially those working in manufacturing and on the customer frontier. They also emphasized the significance of the strong, almost military cultures of Japanese companies.

Corporate America reacted fast. In 1982, Peters and Waterman wrote *In Search of Excellence*, a study of 43 successful American companies, including IBM, McDonald's, Delta, Hewlett-Packard, Wang Labs, TI. Presented as "the art of American management" and with statements such as "good management is resident not only in Japan" and "a host of American companies is doing it right," and discussing "American companies with cultures just as strong as their Japanese counterparts," it was clearly the American answer to *The Art of Japanese Management*. The answer was very American indeed. Peters and Waterman's advice for excellence included a bias for action, strong shared values (but tolerance for employees who accepted these values), and creating an atmosphere to ensure that these employees invested all their efforts in the success of the company by convincing them that they would share in the rewards.

In another influential publication in 1982, *Corporate Cultures*, Deal and Kennedy were even more explicit about the need for a powerful shared culture. Their advice was not to mimic the Japanese: "the solution is as American as apple pie." Their success stories included IBM, Digital, Tandem, P&G, and Continental Bank.

These and other books caused a real corporate culture hype. Para-doxically, they also caused the concept of corporate culture to become discredited a few years later. Although Pascale and Athos had warned that Japanese corporate cultures should not be imitated but used to learn from, many companies tried to copy their practices and found that they did not work in a different context. Moreover, it soon turned out that Japanese companies were not always success-ful, especially not in their globalization processes.

Many of the successes of *In Search of Excellence* turned out not to be enduring. Wang Labs went bankrupt in 1982. In 1984, less than two years after the publication of the book, Business Week published a cover story (Business Week, 1984) revealing that a third of the "excellent companies" were struggling – for example, Eastman Kodak, Westinghouse, Digital, Amdahl, and Data General. Later, other "excellent" companies, such as IBM, went through tough times as well. Some of the successful companies described in Deal and Kennedy's Corporate Cultures turned out not to be so success-ful in the long term too; Digital and Continental Bank, for example, were in the end acquired by their competitors.

Many business analysts and managers concluded that the lack of predictive value in the theories developed in these influential publications confirmed what they had always thought: that corporate culture was a vague and elusive concept. The concept of corporate culture was discredited to some extent for a number of years. But "Japanese management" and "excellence" remained buzzwords and, ten years after the corporate culture hype, there came a new wave of publications trying to link corporate culture to success.

The new corporate culture wave: performing cultures

Harvard Business School researchers Kotter and Heskett reiterated the importance of strong corporate cultures and strong leadership to create these cultures in their 1992 bestseller *Corporate Culture and Performance*. What they added to the "strong culture" concept was that company cultures need to be adaptive and must be strategically aligned to a changing business environment. They advocated a corporate culture in which managers valued all constituencies (customers, stockholders, employees), valued leadership at multiple levels and differentiated between adaptive values and more specific practices. Kotter and Heskett also acknowledged the dilemma of "strong" versus "adaptive" cultures, and looked for solutions in corporate cultures that combined being strong, adaptive, and strategically appropriate. They did not address the issue of how to prevent adaptation leading to diluting a strong corporate culture. Moreover, the three case studies (Hewlett-Packard, ICI, and Nissan) of successful culture change included in their book undermined the predictive value of their theory.

Nissan turned out to be a laggard in comparison with Toyota in the 1990s. The Nissan plant in Zama (Japan), heralded as an example of successful culture change, was closed down in 1995. Nissan made huge losses at the end of the 1990s and was forced into the arms of Renault in 1999.

British chemical conglomerate ICI was also hardly credible as a success story, judging by what ICI's chairman Miller Smith said about his company in 1996: "We have been destroying shareholders' value since 1973" (www.squeaker.net/cems/london/ICI%20Final.ppt).

Hewlett-Packard was mentioned in so many publications in the 1980s and early 90s as an example of a strong, successful culture that it could almost be called a cultural icon. And indeed, in the early 90s, HP's egalitarian, innovative, humanistic, technology-driven corporate culture, characterized by collaborative teamwork, patience, thorough decision making, and persistence was still doing well. But in the second half of the decade the situation started to change. More and more the question of whether HP's conservative and technology-oriented culture was appropriate for the rapidly developing industry which required more of a service orientation was being raised. HP definitely had a strong culture, one which was maybe even too strong. For instance, it did not have a good track record in acquisitions. In the integration process after the acquisition of Apollo in 1989, HP had been too dominant. In 1999, Carly Fiorina was brought in as an outsider CEO to change HP's culture, now described as "inner directed" (Fiorina, 2001). Her personal style was described as "at odds with HP's corporate culture" (Caudron, 2003). One of the main reasons for HP's decision to go for a merger with the so-called "PC Cowboy" Compaq was to create a more performance-oriented culture (Anders, 2003; Burrows, 2003; McShane and Von Glonow, 2003). All of this makes the credibility of HP as an example of a company that successfully combined a strong culture with adaptiveness somewhat doubtful as well.

Lasting cultures

The next attempt to link corporate culture to success was *Built to Last* by Stanford researchers Collins and Porras. Published in 1994, it was one of the most successful management books of the decade. Collins and Porras focused on the successful habits of what they called "visionary companies," companies with a "core purpose" and "core values," very similar to the concept of strong corporate cultures. They reiterated the importance of strong corporate cultures for success in terms of financial results, endurance (to make a company less dependent on one leader), reputation, innovation, and motivation of staff. However they also added the need for companies to be adaptable to the environment: "Companies that enjoy enduring success have core values and a core purpose that remain fixed while their business strategies and practices endlessly adapt to a changing world."

The examples cited by Collins and Porras were mainly American ones such as Hewlett-Packard, Johnson & Johnson, Merck, IBM, Motorola, and the occasional Japanese company, like Sony. Their message was that corporate values should be unique and authentic, as in companies such as Hewlett-Packard with its "HP Way" code of ethics drafted by co-founder David Packard. The corporate philosophy of Johnson & Johnson was another example quoted in *Built to Last*: "The company exists to alleviate pain and disease. We believe that our first responsibility is to doctors, nurses, hospitals, mothers, and all others who use our products."

Built to Last gives many examples of visionary companies with strong cultures, but does not explain how such a culture could be created in a company that does not have it. Moreover, the book seems to promote strong, insular, and almost exclusionary cultures, although it does mention the need to be adaptive and find a balance between stakeholders. IBM, one of the examples of successful visionary companies, is a case in point. *Built to Last* was published just after IBM had made a record operating loss in 1992. Collins and Porras argued that IBM's cult-like culture declined as the company headed towards trouble, and appeared strongest when it attained its greatest success. However this example undermines their whole theory of "strong and adaptable": if adapting to a changing environment resulted in IBM's culture being diluted and diminished, then what was the value of a cult-like culture for enduring success? Collins and Porras promised "a blueprint for building organizations which will prosper into the twenty-first century and beyond." But many of their examples of visionary companies, such as Motorola and Hewlett-Packard, went through hard times at the beginning of the twenty-first century.

Silicon Valley cultures

The success of Silicon Valley companies in the 1990s led to a new attempt to link corporate culture and success (Saxenian, 1994; James, 1998; Lee et al, 2000). Publications such as *Success Secrets from Silicon Valley* (James, 1998) claimed that, "no matter what business you are in," a corporate culture with Silicon Valley characteristics (in contrast to a traditional business culture) would be the recipe for success. Silicon Valley corporate cultures were roughly described as workplaces characterized by the ability to adapt to a changing business environment, team orientation, "service" management style, empowerment, and with employees who were passionate about their work because they believed in the goals of the organization and because their work was their hobby. James's examples of Silicon Valley style companies cover a wide spectrum: Cisco, Microsoft, HP, Sun, Dell, Wang, and Softbank, a set of companies with not much more apparently in common than being in the ICT industry and (in

1998) being successful. IBM and Digital, included on the list of excellent or visionary companies in previous publications, now suddenly found themselves on the list of "traditional" cultures. James's example of successful "cultural reengineering," Wang, was not very convincing. Although it had emerged from bankruptcy in 1992, Wang was in a dire state when it was acquired by its much smaller competitor Getronics in 1999. The Japanese company Softbank, mentioned as an example of the implementation of Silicon Valley culture outside of the US, was also unconvincing. Although once heralded as a visionary of Japan's internet revolution, it was one of the first companies to report heavy losses after the collapse of internet enthusiasm, was shown in retrospect to have destroyed value by investments during the dot-com craze, and was frequently criticized for creative accounting.

Dot-com cultures

Not surprisingly, the dot-com craze presented an opportunity for a renewal of the Silicon Valley recipe. Books such as *Culture.com* (Neuhauser et al, 2000) gave advice on how to create a corporate culture that matched the new dot-com business strategy. The ingredients were not very different from Silicon Valley cultures: speed, risk taking, creativity, informality, being democratic and unconventional, results oriented, learning, having open communications, and accepting mistakes. Unfortunately, many of the companies mentioned as proof of the *Culture.com* recipe for success, such as Lucent, were in serious trouble within a year of its publication.

Disappointment in "new" cultures

On the whole, the new corporate culture wave of the 1990s ended in disappointment. Companies had spent a lot of money on consultants helping them to create value statements and "roll-out" a new culture. Frustration about the lack of return on investments in creating and changing corporate cultures had made many executives cynical. One HR manager of a company that had just gone through a process of identifying new core values, facilitated by external consultants, showed us a list of the "100 most popular core values" that he had compiled from company home pages available on the internet. The "new" core values of his company were on the list already – simply picking and choosing from the list would have saved the company a lot of money. That company was not alone; many have defined new core values which are not very different from those of other companies and are, consequently, not at all authentic. And, just as it had turned out to be impossible to implement Japanese culture in a different context, Silicon Valley and dot-com cultures were also difficult to implement in a different context.

Disappointment in new corporate cultures was not limited to executives. Many employees of such companies were disappointed or downright cynical. "Treating people decently" had been one of the credos of a successful corporate culture in *In Search for Excellence*. Many companies picked "people are our most important asset" or a similar phrase as one of their core values. Silicon Valley cultures had promised "work is fun," "empowerment," and "coaching-style" management. The reality experienced by many employees was downsizing, reengineering, rightsizing, and feeling exploited. It seemed that, while work was supposed to be fun, being available for work 24 hours per day, 7 days a week was becoming the rule for many. "People are our most important asset" was twisted into "money is our most important asset" and empowerment was jokingly explained as "it means that you have two jobs: your own job and your boss's job."

Many customers were alienated too, when corporate values such as "customer orientation" turned out to be meaningless and were more than often interpreted as "squeeze as much money out of the customer as you can." Despite an increasing focus on "shareholder value," many shareholders were also disappointed because strong leadership and strong corporate cultures did not always bring the desired results. The public at large was disappointed because core values such as "community involvement" and "responsible citizenship" did not always bring what they promised.

Back to "strong" cultures?

Some of the instigators of the excitement about corporate culture seemed to share this feeling of disappointment. Collins (*Good to Great*, 2001) and Deal and Kennedy (*The New Corporate Cultures*, 1999) published follow-ups to their bestsellers, basically explaining why the corporate culture concept had not brought the results that they had predicted.

Deal and Kennedy blamed economic ups and downs, in combination with the focus on shareholder value, downsizing, and business process reengineering together with isolation because of new technology, which made it difficult to maintain a cohesive culture over time. Their diagnosis was that corporate cultures had not become stronger but weaker since the publication of their earlier book in 1982. As a remedy, they proposed that companies take measures to make corporate cultures stronger. The risk of this is, of course, that "stronger" corporate cultures would result in even more insular corporate cultures. One of the examples they cite of how to reinforce a company's cultural roots is Arthur Andersen's cultural orientation program – yes, the same company whose downfall in 2002 was blamed on a strong culture that had turned against it because it had resulted in overconfidence and arrogance.

Collins blamed the disappointing results of implementing core values on putting too much emphasis on strong leaders. In *Good to Great* he reports that companies which went through a transformation from being quite ordinary to being great had a few things in common: they did not depend on charismatic leaders but on quietly determined bosses, who combined strong will and humbleness, discipline and entrepreneurship.

CORPORATE CULTURE AS A PROBLEM

Despite these attempts to revitalize the corporate culture wave, several developments make corporate culture look more and more like a problem instead of a success factor.

Firstly, corporate culture clashes in post-merger and acquisition processes, such as in AOL–Time Warner, DaimlerChrysler and Corus (the merger between British Steel and Dutch Hoogovens).

Secondly, corporate scandals related to the occurrence of unhealthy corporate cultures such as at Enron: Enron's core values of integrity, respect, communication, and excellence clearly did not match the behavior of its executives, showing the risk of defining core values which have no meaning because they are not rooted in the basic assumptions of the company. The accounting scandals at WorldCom (filed for bankruptcy in 2002) and Xerox were blamed on corporate cultures that created an illusion of value. In these cases, the corporate culture actually helped in spreading unethical behaviors.

Thirdly, the occurrence of "cultures of entrapment," a term coined by Weick and Sutcliffe (2003). In cultures of entrapment people feel forced to justify inadequate performance. NASA, once heralded for its goal-oriented culture, is a case in point. The board investigating the space shuttle Columbia disaster in 2003 reported that both this incident and the 1986 Challenger shuttle tragedy were a consequence of NASA's organization culture, which led to flawed decision making and to making schedules and budgets more important than safety.

Finally, the tendency among executives to blame corporate culture when strategic initiatives and change initiatives fail. Two consecutive CEOs of Philips Electronics, Jan Timmer (CEO between 1990 and 1996) and Cor Boonstra (CEO between 1996 and 2001), blamed the tenacious "old" culture when their change initiatives – aiming to make Philips more performance oriented and more marketing oriented – did not live up to expectations.

How can it be that corporate culture has turned from a recipe for success to a potential problem? We are now in the position to identify the reasons why linking corporate culture and success has been such a tricky issue – and what the missing links are.

CORPORATE CULTURE AND SUCCESS:
THE MISSING LINKS

Let's look at the "missing links" in detail.

Many proponents of corporate culture as a success factor have confused "strong" cultures with homogeneous or even cult-like cultures.

Strong corporate cultures were presented as a key factor in enhancing competitive performance through greater employee commitment and flexibility. The line of reasoning is basically that employees in strong cultures know what is expected of them; conversely, staff in "weak" cultures supposedly waste time trying to discover this. According to this argument employees identify with a strong culture and take pride in their organization. The pitfall of the argument is that employees who always know exactly what is expected of them will, in the long run, inevitably lose their creativity and initiative. "Strong" was interpreted as "suppress diversity" and "every employee has to adapt to how we do things around here." These cultures will stagnate in the end because people are afraid to voice their opinions and to develop their ideas. Such strong corporate cultures cannot be adaptive. They become proud, insular, and unreceptive to bad news because information does not get through to the right levels. Then the corporate culture becomes an obstacle to change.

In reality, diversity does not have to make organizations weak, it can make them more dynamic. In diverse organizations, trying to discover what is required is not seen as wasting time, but as an opportunity for learning. The issue is not that a company needs to choose between a strong or a weak culture. The issue is how to resolve the dilemma between a homogenous and a differentiated one. Each of these extremes has its downsides. Homogenous cultures tend to end up in cult-like cultures, while differentiated cultures can become fragmented and indecisive. The compromise is a diluted and still not adaptive culture.

Reconciliation of this dilemma leads to a really strong culture: a culture where people show their loyalty to the goals of the organization and their ambition to aim high through speaking their minds, through being critical about behaviors, through ringing warning bells when they disagree with where the organization is going, and through proposing diverging initiatives which can become the new core activity of the company in the long term. In short, the reconciliation between integrated and differentiated cultures are corporate

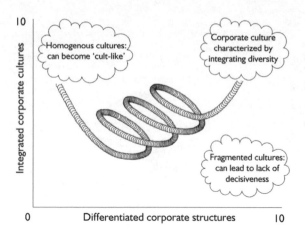

Figure 1.2   The dilemma of integrated versus differentiated corporate cultures

cultures characterized by integrating diversity, as illustrated in Figure 1.2.

The process of achieving and sustaining corporate culture change has been underestimated.

All too often, corporate culture change is presented as discarding the old culture and implementing a completely new one. However, radically changing a corporate culture can be disruptive and lead to throwing away the best of the current culture. Changing organizational cultures is a dilemma in itself. On the one hand, organizational cultures provide a core of the company that is enduring and the strengths of this core need to be kept (stability). On the other hand they need to be adaptable to a changing environment (change). Corporate culture change is not just defining a new set of aspirational values and teaching new behaviors. New, aspirational values need to be combined with preserving the core values rooted in the identity of the company. The tension between the current and the aspired culture needs to be reconciled as in "seek change to preserve continuity." Financial markets cause pressure on companies

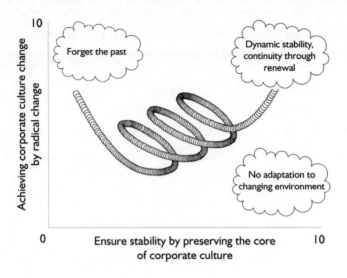

Figure 1.3 The dilemma of change versus continuity in corporate culture

for speedy change and some companies forget their past in the process. The Dutch retail company Ahold forgot its cultural roots in a spree of international acquisitions and was threatened by discontinuity. Apple had forgotten its past after founder Steve Jobs left; the company had three CEOs in four years who did not fit its culture of entrepreneurship and innovation. The return of Steve Jobs in 1997 led to a revitilization of Apple's tradition of building unique computers with the introduction of the iMac. Corporate culture change needs a balance between radical change and organic modifications, bold moves, and incremental adjustment. In a healthy climate for innovation, change is seen as a way of life. The dilemma of change versus stability needs to be reconciled by "dynamic stability" (Abrahamson, 2000) or "continuity through renewal," as in Figure 1.3.

Corporate culture has been used as a tool at the expense of being an authentic representation of what the company really is.

Companies use corporate culture as a tool to improve their reputation as "ethical" companies, as a marketing tool to develop brand identity, or as a tool to attract talented people in the war for talent. Although it is true that it becomes more and more important to let customers, communities, and (prospective) employees know who you are and what you stand for, using corporate culture as a tool may lead to defining a corporate culture that is not authentic, with values that are not meaningful, and hollow purpose statements. A company that claims to have "integrity" or to value "teamwork" or other politically correct terms will not be credible unless these claims are supported by concrete action. Lack of support of values by action may actually damage the company's culture and will make people cynical. Reputation can disappear more quickly than it has been acquired. Developing meaningful corporate values is a process of finding out what the company stands for, making a commitment to be serious about it and "walking the talk." Corporate values must provide answers to some of the fundamental dilemmas the company is facing. They need to help in making day-to-day decisions, and will therefore be controversial, instigate debate, and – possibly – cause pain. Developing meaningful corporate values is a process of constructive confrontation, as illustrated in Figure 1.4.

Descriptions of "ideal" or "excellent" corporate cultures reflect what was in vogue at the time of their publication.

So, over time, the "ideal" has shifted from a people-oriented culture, inspired by Japanese corporate culture characteristics, to strong leadership cultures and high performance cultures inspired by successful mainstream American businesses, and then to the flexible

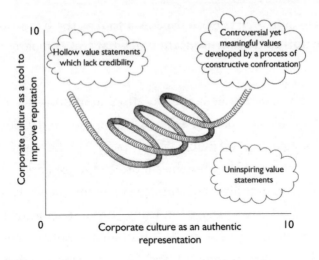

Figure 1.4   The dilemma of developing corporate culture values

and entrepreneurial cultures of Silicon Valley and the dot-com world. Over time, the proposed ideal corporate cultures swung back and forth between extreme value orientations such as focusing on shareholder value versus focusing on building a long-term, open, trusting, and learning corporate culture. Cultures based on extreme value orientations can be successful over a limited period in a certain context, but sooner or later the downside of these extreme value orientations will become dominant. For enduring success, corporate culture needs to help the company in resolving the dilemmas it is facing in internal clashes and external adaptation, in line with our earlier definition of corporate culture as the pattern by which value differences are habitually mediated within a company. A long-term, viable corporate culture must explicitly address the tension and find the balance between seemingly contradictory values, as in for example "enhance shareholders value while building a high involvement listening, learning, responsive organization," as in Figure 1.5.

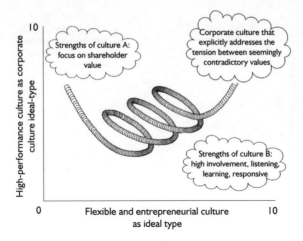

Figure 1.5 The dilemma between the different "ideal" types of corporate culture

The impact of globalization on corporate cultures has been underestimated.

The focus in linking corporate culture to success has been on lessons learnt from corporate cultures successful in more or less homogenous environments (e.g., Japanese corporate culture, "mainstream" American corporate culture, and even Silicon Valley corporate cultures although these already operate in a more diverse environment). The impact of globalization is that most companies must be successful in environments with more cultural diversity. That does not work with a corporate culture based on a set of values that only fits in one culture. For instance, Canon had a lot of problems in translating its Kyosei philosophy ("working for the common good") to its western staff. The issue then becomes one of how to reconcile dilemmas coming from value differences between the place where the company has it roots and where it is operating. The well known phrase "think global, act local" is not a reconciliation, but a mere compromise. It is often interpreted as "we (at headquarters) do

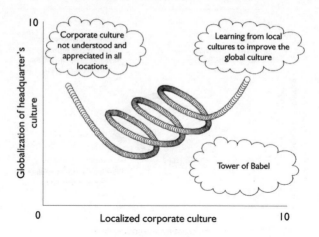

Figure 1.6 The dilemma of corporate culture and globalization

the thinking and you (the local staff) do the work." Reconciliation involves "learning from local cultural values to improve the global corporate culture," as is depicted in Figure 1.6.

The intangible aspects of corporate culture have been underestimated.

Consultancy companies have been instrumental in trying to create "value-driven organizations" by defining "core values" and rigidly translating these to "leadership competencies" and "preferred behaviors" which can be measured and assessed. It tends to be forgotten that people need to form an emotional tie to a corporate culture in order to create the desired "networks of meaning." In our experience it is a more effective approach to give people the opportunity to discuss the dilemmas that they face when they want to "live" the core values in day-to-day behavior and practices. This leads to a dialogue which helps managers in understanding the deeply rooted assumptions and perceptions in the company and in changing day-to-day behaviors (Figure 1.7).

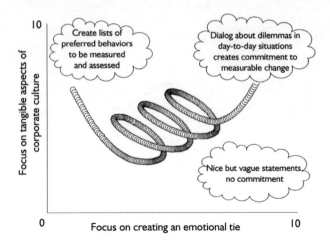

Figure 1.7 The dilemma between tangible and untangible aspects of corporate culture

In the following chapters we will develop a conceptual model and an approach to culture change and integration that addresses these "missing links." First we will review the existing models for understanding corporate cultures.

CHAPTER 2

Existing models for understanding and mapping corporate cultures

Developing a reconciling corporate culture starts with understanding where your corporate culture is now, and that is where models of corporate culture can help.

Over time, several frameworks, models, and typologies have been developed to distinguish between different corporate cultures: that is, to identify the differences between basic assumptions of different types of companies. Many of these models take the form of 2 × 2 matrices, distinguishing two sets of value polarities (or "dimensions of culture") leading to four types of corporate culture. We will first look at the model that we have successfully used for many years to distinguish corporate cultures in our consulting practice at THT and then look at how other models (Quinn, Deal and Kennedy, Goffee and Jones, Hofstede) can add to understanding the corporate cultures of modern corporations.

THE TROMPENAARS CORPORATE CULTURE MODEL: TOWARDS GUIDED INCUBATORS?

The Trompenaars model of corporate culture (described in detail in Trompenaars and Hampden-Turner, 1997, 2003) is a 2 × 2 matrix of corporate culture types. It is the result of a unique set of combinations of the seven dimensions of culture as defined in *Riding the Waves of Culture* (Trompenaars and Hampden-Turner, 1997), which distinguishes seven fundamental value orientations (Trompenaars and Woolliams, 2003). However, it is focuses primarily on two value dimensions: person oriented versus task oriented, and hierarchical versus egalitarian. The first dimension is related to the universal and specific versus particularistic and diffuse dimension, and the second – hierarchical versus egalitarian – dimension is related to the achievement versus ascription dimension of the seven dimensions model. These two dimensions were chosen as the basis of the

Trompenaars corporate culture model because they cover many important differences between corporate cultures.

The 2 × 2 matrix leads to four types of corporate culture, as shown in Figure 2.1:

- The Eiffel Tower
- The Family
- The Incubator
- The Guided Missile

First, let's briefly examine the four types.

The Incubator (top left quadrant), typical of Silicon Valley, is a culture which is both person oriented and egalitarian. The purpose of such a culture is to free individuals from performing routine tasks in order to enable the highly creative "incubating" of new ideas. Such organizations are egalitarian because anyone, at any moment and

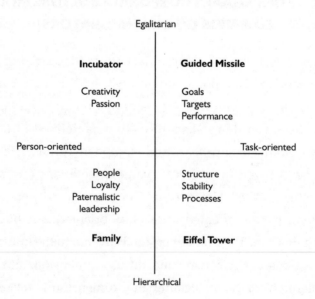

Figure 2.1 The Trompenaars corporate culture model – four corporate culture typologies, including keywords for each quadrant

regardless of their status, may come up with a winning idea. They are person-oriented cultures, because their essence is the creativity, passion, and improvisation skills of individuals. Work satisfaction in this type of corporate culture is based on continuous learning, passion for the work itself, and celebrating new discoveries.

The Guided Missile (top right quadrant) is an egalitarian, task-oriented culture devoted to the accomplishment of tasks, goals, and targets, which are often undertaken by project groups. These are typically multi-disciplinary, taking from the various functions of the organization exactly those people essential for completing their set task. Guided Missile cultures are egalitarian because people are evaluated on what they can contribute to the team and on their performance, and not on any status which is ascribed to them based on other criteria. Work satisfaction in this type of corporate culture is based on the (material) reward attached to the completed task.

The Eiffel Tower culture (bottom right quadrant) is highly structured, as in the case of a factory processing physical materials; in the case of a large bureaucracy it does precise, detailed, and routine tasks without error. Everyone has a precise job description, even if it's only fixing mirrors to a succession of automobiles on an assembly line. Bosses have the authority to order employees to work according to their clear instructions. The culture is stable, predictable, safe, routine, and reliable. Work satisfaction in this type of corporate culture is based on building competence in a well-defined area.

The Family culture (bottom left quadrant) is a term used to describe a culture which is at the same time personal, with close face-to-face relations, but also hierarchical, in the sense that the gap between "parents" as owners (or managers) and "children" as employees is very wide. The result is a power-oriented corporate culture in which leaders are regarded as caring parents who know better than their employees what should be done and what is good for them. These powerful leaders may be revered or feared. This type of culture can be found in actual family companies and in companies that originate from family enterprises, but publicly owned companies may have a family atmosphere as well. The family culture is personal rather than task oriented, because who you are is more important than what you do. Work satisfaction in this type of corporate culture is based on loyalty and the accumulation of power and status over time.

The strengths and weaknesses of each corporate culture type

It is important to realize that none of the four corporate culture types in Figure 2.1 is an ideal model. Each type has its strengths and weaknesses. Now let's look at these.

The strengths of Incubator cultures are flexibility, improvisation, innovation, adaptability, and responsiveness. In addition they are people driven and capitalise on people skills, they seize opportunities and do not shy off from taking intuitive decisions; they also encourage networking and promote commitment and passion for work.

The weaknesses of these cultures are that there can be a lack of commitment to common goals and that they can be chaotic and lead to confusion: a lack of formal systems may lead to duplication of efforts. Incubators can also be overly dependent on specific, creative individuals and make it difficult for these people to find a proper work/life balance. Furthermore, because of the close personal relationships involved, it may be difficult for people to criticize each other.

The strengths of Guided Missile cultures are clarity, transparency, predictability, having structured processes, and being controllable, task focused, objectives driven, and (in at least the short term) results oriented. They tend to promote drive and mobility.

Their weaknesses are that there can be a lack of long-term orientation, a lack of trust, of creativity, of loyalty, an obsession with numbers and systems, too much focus on self-interest, and an atmosphere of fear.

The strengths of Family cultures are loyalty, trust, decisiveness, and long-term orientation.

Their weaknesses are a lack of clarity and systems, an overreliance on hierarchy, status, specific powerful individuals, and over-centralization. They may also lead to power games, "groupthink," and a lack of openness because people do not dare to speak their minds.

The strengths of Eiffel Tower cultures are efficiency, stability, and professionalism.

Their weaknesses are that they can be machine-like, overly structured, overly managed, and controlled, rigid, slow, uninspiring, and demotivating for individuals. Plans, systems, procedures, and processes become more important than goals.

At THT we have used this corporate culture model in our consulting practice to construct the corporate culture profile of numerous international companies. We use a questionnaire which asks respondents to make a choice between four statements in order to evaluate which of the four corporate culture types comes closest to the respondent's own corporate culture. Respondents are asked to do this for what they believe the current situation to be in their organizations, and for what they believe would be the ideal situation.

We assess their corporate culture profile by evaluating the answers on four statements of choice, in which each choice corresponds with one of the quadrants of the model, like this:

(a)   Working effectively means that both the individual members and the company agree upon objectives and that people are given the freedom to attain these goals.

(b)   Working effectively means that the manager gives the objectives and directs the members of the department in fulfilling the various tasks that need to be done.

(c)   Working effectively means that the objectives and the roles to fulfill them are clearly described, even in cases where they obstruct individual freedom and inventiveness.

(d)   Working effectively means that the individual members feel challenged by the task at hand.

Answer (a) represents a Guided Missile culture; answer (b) represents a Family culture; answer (c) represents an Eiffel Tower culture and answer (d) represents an Incubator. Figure 2.2 shows a graphic presentation of current and ideal culture derived from this assessment.

The example in Figure 2.2 represents the single most frequently occurring situation: where respondents want to get rid of all hierarchy and where their preferred ideal model is a "guided incubator." This reveals a limitation to this type of corporate culture assessment: people perceive only the negative sides of the Family and the Eiffel Tower, and the positive aspects of the Guided Missile and Incubator. Moreover, we force the respondents to choose extreme value orien-

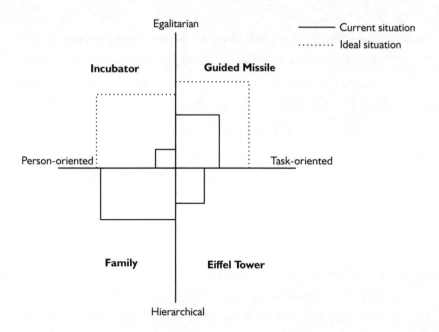

Figure 2.2 Trompenaars model: Corporate culture assessment

tations, while the assessment shows that there is a perceived need to reconcile at least the Incubator and Guided Missile cultures.

This model has proved valuable for assessing corporate cultures. However we are now in a position to evaluate how it can be improved.

- Our assessment did not distinguish between organizations that combine the positive characteristics of a certain corporate culture type and organizations that combine the negative characteristics of that corporate culture type. In real life there are well-targeted Guided Missiles and mis-Guided Missiles. There are vibrant and energetic Incubators and chaotic Incubators. There are happy Families and problem Families. There are Eiffel Towers that reach for the sky and Eiffel Towers that are vulnerable because of their rigidity. It seems that almost every company nowadays looks for the ideal of combining the goal-oriented Guided Missile and the passionate, entrepreneurial Incubator. What tends to be forgotten is that such a "guided incubator" will not be sustainable without Family and Eiffel Tower strengths such as loyalty, trust, decisiveness related to authority, long-term orientation, and stability.

- The interaction between a company and its environment has become more and more important for distinguishing corporate cultures: to what extent a company is responsive to customers, to what extent a company focuses on short-term shareholder value versus long-term value for all stakeholders, and how a company interacts with its competition. For instance, different types of Incubators can be distinguished, although they all fit within the egalitarian/person oriented quadrant. There are short-term oriented Incubators, with a focus on quick and strong market presence, hoping for a cash-out such as an IPO or acquisition by an established player. Internet start-up Worldonline comes to mind here. There are also long-term oriented Incubators, created by leaders who look for others who share their passion and who want to create a company with deeply held values – a bit like Hewlett-Packard in its early days.

- The four quadrants represent different combinations of two extreme value orientations. Maximizing one quadrant means maximizing the extreme end of these value orientations, while avoiding the opposite end. However, in line with our definition of corporate culture, the challenge is not to embrace one quadrant or one set of value orientations. The art of creating a viable corporate culture is to reconcile these seemingly opposing value orientations or dilemmas. The challenge is to build authority through empowerment, to stimulate teamwork through individual incentives, to show courage through taking calculated risks, and to become consistent through learning from exceptional situations.

Embracing one set of value orientations as an ideal corporate culture is exactly the pitfall of equating strong corporate cultures with homogenous cultures. Many of the examples in Pascale and Athos's *Art of Japanese Management* embrace the Family corporate culture as the ideal model. Many of Peters and Waterman's "excellent companies," Collins and Porras's "visionary companies with big hairy audacious goals," and Kotter and Heskett's "high performance organizations" embrace the Guided Missile culture as the ideal. The publications heralding Silicon Valley cultures and dot-com cultures all embrace the Incubator model. In the strong corporate culture concept, mixing a strong culture with other models is seen as diluting the culture, something that needs to be avoided. Although each of these extreme models or types can indeed be successful for a certain time and in a certain context, maximizing one of the quadrants will inevitably lead, in the end, to "cultural lock-in," and will uncover the weaknesses of each quadrant. We'll develop the concept of the "reconciling corporate culture" further in Chapter 3.

• The assessment gives one overall evaluation of the corporate culture type. Currently, companies interested in an assessment of their corporate cultures demand that the assessment gives detailed input, for instance in order to guide corporate culture change. This means that corporate culture assessment must address all the key elements of corporate culture in detail.

The nine dimensions of corporate culture

We can address these key elements by looking at all the corporate culture dilemmas that are implicit in the corporate culture model of

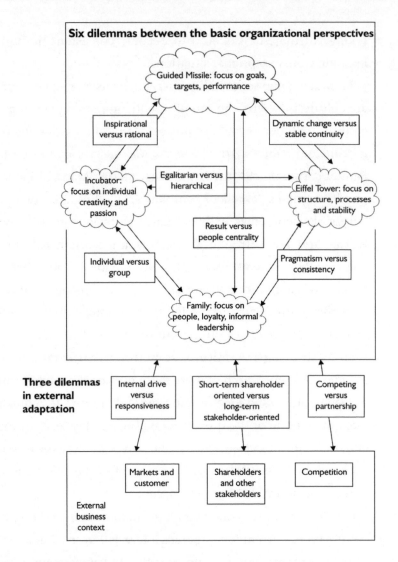

Figure 2.3 The nine dilemmas of corporate culture

Figure 2.1 and the dilemmas of external adaptation. Figure 2.3 shows that the four organizational perspectives, represented by the major corporate cultures, lead to six dilemmas. The first six dilemmas are:

- pragmatism versus consistency,
- individual versus group,

- result versus people centrality,
- egalitarian versus hierarchical,
- inspirational versus rational, and
- dynamic change versus stable continuity.

It also shows that three main dilemmas of external adaptation can be distinguished – one related to adaptation to markets and customers, one related to adaptation to shareholders and other stakeholders, and one related to adaptation to the competition. These three dilemmas are:

- internal drive versus responsiveness,
- short-term, shareholder oriented versus long-term, stakeholder oriented, and
- competing versus partnership.

These nine dilemmas can be brought together in a model of nine corporate culture dimensions, shown in Figure 2.3.

The nine corporate culture dilemmas or dimensions are all manifestations of the dimensions of the Trompenaars seven dimensions model of cultural values, when we take the two subdimensions of the seven dimensions model into account. Each of the nine dimensions is directly related to a key element of corporate culture, allowing detailed corporate culture assessments. Let's look at this in more detail.

Universalism versus particularism

In universalistic cultures there is an obligation to the standards which are universally agreed in that culture. In particularist cultures there are particular obligations to people and unique situations. This has an impact on corporate culture in terms of of how a company is organized through systems, structure, procedures, and accountabilities. The first dimension of corporate culture is *consistency versus pragmatism.*

Individualism versus communitarianism

Do people regard themselves primarily as individuals, focusing on their own individual interests, or do they regard themselves primarily as part of a group, focusing on common goals and objectives? This has an impact on corporate culture in terms of how individuals are integrated into groups in the company and influences rewarding, motivating, teamwork, and sharing knowledge. The second dimension of corporate culture is *individualism versus group orientation.*

Specific versus diffuse

Specific versus diffuse stands for segregating phenomena into parts versus integrating these phenomena into complete patterns. Specific cultures emphasize facts, units, analysis, and hard numbers. In terms of business relationships, each interaction stands alone in the specific situation of the present moment. Diffuse cultures emphasize relations, patterns, connectedness, synthesis, and "soft" processes. In terms of business relationships, one interaction cannot be separated from its context because once the relationship is built, it is a deeper, all-encompassing one. This impacts on corporate culture in terms of how the company deals with its competitors, customers, and suppliers. The third dimension of corporate culture is *competing versus partnership orientation.*

There is another corporate culture dimension related to the specific–diffuse dichotomy. In specific cultures, task and person can be seen as separate. In diffuse cultures, task and person cannot be separated. This has an impact on corporate culture in terms of how members of an organization are perceived. Are employees seen as human resources and do work relations tend to be task oriented, or is business a human affair in which organizational members are flesh and blood and work relations are rather more people oriented? This has an impact on corporate culture issues such as people development, conflict handling, relationships, and building trust. The fourth dimension of corporate culture is *result centrality versus people centrality.*

Neutral versus affective

Should the nature of business be rational and detached, or is the role of emotions, intuition, etc., accepted? This has an impact on corporate culture in terms of how people communicate and on ways of thinking. The fifth dimension of corporate culture is *rational versus inspirational.*

Achievement versus ascription

In achievement-oriented cultures, employees are treated on the basis of equality in order to elicit from them the best they have to give. In ascription-oriented cultures the emphasis is on the judgement and authority of the hierarchy, who coach and evaluate the employees. This impacts on corporate culture in terms of how hierarchical relationships are handled: leadership style, decision making, and corporate governance. The sixth dimension of corporate culture is *egalitarian versus hierarchical.*

Internal versus external control

Internal control orientation stands for influencing or even dominating the environment by imposing your will on it, using your power to overcome the obstacles. External control orientation stands for accepting the unpredictable, uncontrollable forces, and developments in the environment and responding to them. This has an impact on corporate culture in terms of how the company deals with uncertainty and ambiguity in its (market) environment. Does it deal with uncertainty and ambiguity by an assertive or even aggressive attitude, trying to influence and dominate the environment, or does it take a more accommodating attitude in trying to respond to changing market conditions? The seventh dimension of corporate culture is *internal drive versus responsiveness.*

How we deal with time

The cultural dimension of orientation towards time has two distinct subdimensions. The first one deals with the way in which cultures organize time: sequentially and synchronically organized activities. Cultures with a sequential orientation view time as a consecutive series of events coming at regular intervals. Sequential people are distressed if they are thrown off schedule by anything unexpected happening. They are more comfortable with detailed planning schedules and stable continuity. In cultures with a synchronic orientation, past, present, and future are all interrelated and time is conceived of as cyclical. For synchronic people, change and renewal are a way of life; they take a more dynamic view of time. This has an impact on corporate culture in terms of how the company deals with change. The eighth dimension of corporate culture is *stable continuity versus dynamic change.*

The second corporate culture dimension related to time deals with differences in orientation to past, present, and future: short-term oriented cultures (focused on the here and now and short-term growth) versus long-term oriented cultures. This has an impact on corporate culture in terms of how the company deals with the short-term interests of its shareholders versus the long-term interests of all stakeholders. The ninth dimension of corporate culture is *short-term orientation versus long-term orientation.*

In Chapter 3 we will show that all these nine dimensions are relevant for understanding corporate cultures.

OTHER CORPORATE CULTURE MODELS AND TYPOLOGIES

Quinn: competing values

Quinn is one of the few authors on organizational analysis who has emphasized that organizations need to balance and simultaneously master seemingly contradictory or paradoxical capabilities. Quinn's "competing values" model acknowledges the continuous tension between competing values because of internal competition, external competition, and market developments. Cameron and Quinn (1999) have applied this competing values framework to corporate culture. They also distinguish two dimensions of corporate culture and emphasize the need to find a balance between the competing values of each dimension:

- control versus flexibility
- internal focus (focus on internal processes) versus external focus (focus on markets and stakeholders).

Quinn's model leads, like the Trompenaars model, to a 2 × 2 matrix and four corporate culture types (Figure 2.4): the Clan (internal focus/flexibility), the Adhocracy (external focus/flexibility), the Hierarchy (internal focus/control) and the Market (external focus/control). Although there are similarities between Quinn's model and the Trompenaars corporate culture model in Figure 2.1,

Figure 2.4 Quinn model of corporate culture (after Cameron and Quinn, 1999)

there are differences as well. Quinn's dimension of control versus flexibility is very similar to the consistency versus pragmatism dimension in our corporate culture model. Quinn's internal focus versus external focus dimension is related to the THT internal drive versus responsiveness dimension: a focus on imposing internal processes on the environment versus a focus on identifying market needs and responding to these.

But, as noted, there are differences. For instance, the four corporate culture types are not completely equivalent to the types in the Trompenaars model. As an example, although a company that fits Quinn's Clan type of corporate culture can be similar to the hierarchical Family culture in the Trompenaars model, the Clan corporate culture also encompasses a more egalitarian, network type of organization, emphasizing participation, empowerment, and consensus.

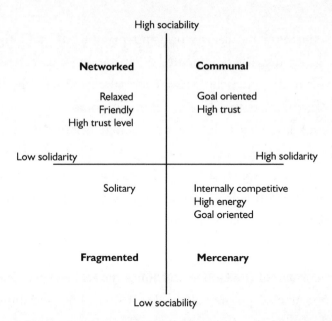

Figure 2.5   Goffee and Jones model of corporate culture (after Goffee and Jones, 1996)

Goffee and Jones

Goffee and Jones published their corporate culture model in a *Harvard Business Review* article in 1996. Their model, which has been used by consultancy companies, uses two types of human relations to build a corporate culture model: solidarity (the ability to pursue shared goals) and sociability (the level of warmth and friendliness among employees). Distinguishing between low solidarity versus high solidarity and between low sociability versus high sociability leads to another 2 × 2 matrix and four corporate culture types: Networked, Communal, Mercenary, and Fragmented corporate cultures (Figure 2.5).

The Networked company is characterized by a relaxed and friendly atmosphere and a high level of trust. The Mercenary company is focused on business matters, and is characterized by quick decisions, separation between work and private life, and fighting against the enemy. The Fragmented organization is characterized by high levels of dissent; people may even sabotage each other in this type of organization, which can be found in some consultancy companies and law firms. In the Communal organization people combine friendships, trust, mutually beneficial objectives, and goals. Communal organizations combine high trust and goal orientation, but are difficult to sustain during periods of change and globalization, when the organization needs focus, urgency, and performance.

The dimensions of the Goffee and Jones model are very similar to two of our nine corporate culture dimensions. Low sociability versus high sociability (level of warmth and friendliness among employees) is related to our result centrality versus people centrality dimension. Low solidarity versus high solidarity is related to the individualism versus group orientation dimension.

Deal and Kennedy

While the Trompenaars model of culture was originally developed to understand national cultural differences, and Quinn together with Goffee and Jones view organizations from a sociological perspective, Deal and Kennedy (1982) base their corporate culture model on differences between business environments. They distinguish between business environments with fast versus slow feedback and business environments which require high levels of risk taking versus those with low levels of risk taking. That leads to another 2 × 2 matrix with four corporate culture types, each quadrant fitting certain industries (Figure 2.6).

Although the high risk–low risk and fast feedback–slow feedback dichotomies are not really cultural dimensions (they define different

High risk

Tough-guy macho culture

Entertainment industry
Software industry
Investment banking
Management consulting

Bet your company culture

Oil companies
Aircraft manufacturers
Capital goods

Fast feedback   Slow feedback

Sales organisations
Office equipment
Computer companies

Banks
Insurance companies
Accounting firms

Work hard/play hard culture

Process culture

Low risk

Figure 2.6 Deal and Kennedy model for corporate culture (after Deal and Kennedy, 1982)

business contexts which may lead to different orientations on corporate culture dimensions) it is easy to see that the contexts distinguished by Deal and Kennedy are associated with our two corporate culture dimensions related to time.

The fast feedback–slow feedback dimension is related to our short term versus long term orientation. Companies in a fast feedback environment tend to develop a short-term oriented corporate culture. Companies in a slow feedback environment tend to develop a longer-term oriented corporate culture.

The high risk–low risk dimension is related to our dimension of dynamic change versus stable continuity. In a high risk environment, companies develop a culture that can handle dynamic change. In a low risk environment, companies develop a culture characterized by stable continuity.

Although Deal and Kennedy's model is presented as one covering all possible corporate cultures, it is very much limited to the American business environment. Their corporate culture types are limited to the "internal drive" orientation (influence the environment and use power to overcome obstacles) and miss out on the "responsiveness" orientation (accommodate to the forces in the environment). The labels for their corporate culture types all fit this internal drive orientation. The model assumes that all companies in a high risk environment tend to try to manage risk by dominating that environment: taking an aggressive, competitive approach to create a market. This fits the Tough Guy, Macho culture and the Bet Your Company culture labels. The model also assumes that companies in a low risk environment either display the self-confidence and self-directness to push their products/services (fitting the action-oriented, Work Hard/Play Hard culture) or focus on stable, orderly internal processes and imposing these on their customers (fitting the Process culture label). They forget that companies in high risk and low risk environments can also have a responsiveness corporate culture, focused on finding market needs and responding to these, and adapting to competitors' efforts as well as to uncontrollable developments such as changing exchange and interest rates. This would lead to corporate culture types with less "arrogant" labels, for example, a service-oriented culture.

Hofstede

Hofstede (1991) states that two of his dimensions of national culture have an impact for organizational culture as well: power distance and uncertainty avoidance. This leads to another 2 × 2 matrix and four types of corporate culture: the Pyramid, the Machine, the Family and the Village Market (Figure 2.7). We disagree with Hofstede because we do not consider low versus high uncertainty to be a fun-

Figure 2.7 Hofstede model of corporate culture (after Hofstede, 1991)

damental cultural dimension. Organizational cultures do not differ in high and low uncertainty avoidance, but in how they avoid that uncertainty. Several cultural dimensions play a role in describing different ways of avoiding uncertainty.

All the organizational culture types that Hofstede mentions have their ways of avoiding uncertainty but the main mechanism for doing so is different. In Machine corporate cultures uncertainty is avoided by making detailed long-term plans, procedures, and rules (consistency). In Pyramid corporate cultures, uncertainty is avoided by creating stable hierarchical structures and procedures for collecting information (stable continuity). In his Family corporate cultures, uncertainty is avoided by relying on the decisiveness of powerful leaders (hierarchical). In Village Market corporate cultures, uncertainty is avoided by trying to take control of the environment by creating markets (internal drive).

All these different ways of avoiding uncertainty are covered by cultural dimensions incorporated in our model, that is consistency versus pragmatism, hierarchy versus egalitarianism, internal drive versus responsiveness, stable continuity versus dynamic change. Hofstede's other dimension, power distance, is also covered by our model in the hierarchical versus egalitarian dimension. As a result we conclude that Hofstede's model has limited value for understanding differences between corporate cultures; the fact that Denmark, the Netherlands, the UK and the US all end up in the same quadrant of his model shows that it is not sufficiently discriminating.

Sanders and Neuijen

In their IRIC study of organizational culture (detailed in Hofstede *et al.*, 1990), Sanders and Neuijen found six dimensions of organizational culture, which they labeled as:

- process versus result oriented (similar to our stable continuity versus dynamic change dimension)
- normative versus pragmatic (similar to our consistency versus pragmatism dimension)
- loose control versus tight control (similar to our egalitarian versus hierarchical dimension)
- parochial versus professional (similar to our people centrality versus result centrality dimension)
- open versus closed (similar to our individualism versus group oriented dimension)
- employee versus job oriented (which is similar to some other aspects of our people centrality versus result centrality dimension).

Hofstede, who acted as the academic supervisor of this IRIC study, emphasizes that, when discussing these dimensions, "which position is more or less desirable is a matter of strategic choice, which will vary from one organization to the other" (Hofstede, 2001). The concept of reconciling cultural dilemmas is missing in this way of thinking.

Other models

Even the Myers–Briggs type indicator, a psychometric instrument widely used in business for personality profiling, has been used to measure "corporate personality." In *Companies are People Too* (Fekete, 2003) organizations are labeled according to their position on the four dimensions of the Myers-Briggs instrument:

- Intuition versus sensing
- Introversion versus extroversion
- Feeling versus analytical thinking
- Perceiving (spontaneous, flexible) versus judging (orderly and disciplined).

In using an instrument meant for personality profiling to measure corporate personality, leaders' personalities are inevitably mixed up with corporate cultures. However, the reason that this assessment instrument received some attention is probably that the Myers–Briggs type indicator does address one aspect of business that is not included in most corporate culture models: intuition versus sensing, which is included in our inspirational versus rational corporate culture dimension. As a dimension of corporate culture, inspirational versus rational is especially relevant for understanding the cultures of start-up companies, where the values of leaders have a strong influence on corporate culture.

This review of existing corporate culture models confirms that our nine dimension model covers all relevant aspects of corporate culture. The dimensions of the Trompenaars corporate culture model in Figure 2.1, the Quinn model in Figure 2.4, the Goffee and Jones model in Figure 2.5, the model of Deal and Kennedy shown in Figure 2.6 all together correspond with eight of our nine corporate culture dimensions, and the application of the Myers-Briggs type indicator suggests an additional dimension that corresponds with the ninth dimension of our model.

It also reveals that the concept of looking at corporate culture values as dilemmas that need to be reconciled is new, although it is anticipated by Quinn's competing values model. We are now in the position to develop the nine dimension corporate culture model and the concept of the reconciling corporate culture further.

CHAPTER 3

The reconciling corporate culture: reconciling nine dimensions of corporate culture

We have identified four factors that have prompted us to develop a new conceptual model for describing and understanding corporate cultures:

- The need to distinguish the positive and negative aspects of a corporate culture type.
- The need to evaluate not just the score of a corporate culture on a value orientation, but the extent to which the corporate culture values are reconciled.
- The need for companies to be able to link corporate culture assessment in a practical way to business issues and changing specific elements of corporate culture.
- The need to distinguish between more different types of corporate cultures than the four types of the existing models.

All these factors can be addressed by using the full nine dimensions of corporate culture framework in combination with the concept of the reconciling corporate culture. The nine dimensions are family resemblances of the dimensions we have distinguished in our work on national cultural differences. Initially, let's look in more detail at the nine dimensions of corporate culture, each one of which represents a key dilemma that every corporate culture has to reconcile.

LINKING THE NINE DIMENSIONS OF CORPORATE CULTURE TO CORPORATE ISSUES

Consistency versus pragmatism

This dimension of corporate culture is about valuing consistency by having standardized systems and procedures versus valuing pragmatism by allowing flexibility and adaptation. This is the corporate version of universal versus particular issues. Here the practical business issues are several. One is how a company globalizes: Does it implement standardized systems and procedures worldwide or does it localize as much as possible? This has, for instance, an impact on a preference for establishing global (or regional) shared service centres versus a preference for ensuring local support. There is also how the company is structured. Is this according to a rigid description of the roles of employees in the organization, or is it constructed around the talents and skills of its employees? How does the company deal with integrity? The dilemma here lies between a dogmatic approach, specifying all rules in codes of conduct and codes of ethics, versus a pragmatic approach, giving overall guidelines and implementing them with discretion.

The basic idea of reconciling this dimension is to learn from (local) exceptions to improve global or corporate systems.

Individualism versus group orientation

This dimension of corporate culture is about the degree to which individuals are integrated into groups within the company. Practical business issues are reward systems and knowledge management. The basic assumption in individualistic corporate cultures (such as those of many American companies) is that managers and employees can not be trusted to do their jobs (i.e., increasing shareholder value) unless their interests and the interests of shareholders are aligned by making stock options and individual performance incentives an important part of compensation. In individualistic corporate cultures, knowledge is seen as something that individuals can make explicit by putting in databases; it can be transferred by formal education and training. In group-oriented cultures knowledge is seen as tacit and innate, and can be shared by informal group processes. The basic idea of reconciling this dimension is to reward individuals for what they contribute to groups and to reward groups for how they nurture individual development and initiative.

Competing versus partnership orientation

This particular dimension is about seeing business as a world of competing rivals versus seeing business as a world of cooperation and partnerships. The practical business issues related to this dimension lie in how the company deals with competition, and with customers and suppliers. In competing cultures the attitude to competitors is aggressive, as on a battlefield: it is all about winning market share from opponents and about who is eaten and who does the eating, so that speed is of the essence in the mergers and acquisitions game in order to survive and be successful. This leads to the culture of aggressive acquisition machines such as WorldCom. In competing cultures the attitude to customers and suppliers is all about value in monetary terms. In partnership cultures, the focus is on aligning corporate capabilities with the capabilities of competitors and suppliers. Partnership-oriented companies recognize that they are embedded in a complex ecosystem where having the right connections can mean the difference between success and failure. This leads to different forms of cooperation with suppliers, customers, and competitors, where knowledge sharing, outsourcing, and alliances become more important. In partnership cultures relationships are more personalized and loyalty still counts. The basic idea for reconciling this dimension is co-opetition: cooperate to compete.

People centrality versus result centrality

This dimension of corporate culture is about how organizational members are seen on the broader human versus the specific work areas. Are they people who want to live a meaningful organizational life or are they just a resource hired to do what the company wants them to do? The main business issue related to this dimension is to what extent the organization is committed to its employees. In people centrality cultures there is more attention paid to employee welfare, quality of life, and people development; there is more tolerance of making mistakes and result-focused approaches are less accepted. The balanced scorecard offers ways to reconcile this dimension by taking financial performance and factors such as the welfare of employees and people motivation and development into account when assessing managers. In a reconciling corporate culture, people will identify the organization's needs and goals with their own personal needs and goals.

Rational versus inspirational

This dimension distinguishes rational, analytical, and detached cultures from cultures in which there is a place for intuition, emotions, and passion; this obviously relates to our neutral–affective distinction, as described in Chapter 2. It is about seeing people acting as rational beings and taking decisions based on careful analysis of all available information versus (as often happens in practice) taking decisions based on intuition. It is also about how people communicate and relate to each other in the company: in a rational and detached way, keeping work and private life separate, or in a more emotional way, with less separation between work and private life. The business issue is in to what extent emotions may play a role in communication, decision making, and conflict handling. In a reconciling corporate culture, rational goals are pursued through inspirational leadership.

Egalitarian versus hierarchical

This dimension distinguishes more egalitarian cultures, based on achievements with relatively flat hierarchies, from hierarchical cultures with relatively steep hierarchies derived from attributed status such as seniority and role. The main business issues related to this dimension are leadership styles and ways of decision making. Egalitarian cultures value delegating responsibility and involvement in decision making by a consensus process. Hierarchical cultures give status to leaders based on their hierarchical positions and titles so that they can act with authority and decisiveness. The challenge here is to establish a corporate culture which establishes decisiveness through consensus processes, and in which leaders use their status to coach and help capable people achieve their best.

Internal drive versus responsiveness

This dimension of corporate culture is about influencing and controlling the environment versus responding to the environment and the needs of customers. The practical business issue is the attitude of a company towards its markets and customers: focus on pushing products and technologies versus realizing customers' specific wishes. The risk of the internal drive culture is that it is perceived as arrogant and bullying. Here Customer Relationship Marketing is interpreted as how we can select the customers who deliver most value for us. For instance, in some telecommunication companies, subscribers to services are depersonalized and simply called "subs." Microsoft is an example of a company with an aggressive market approach and an effective monopoly in its market of operating systems and application software. Responsiveness cultures try to align core capabilities with the needs of customers and attempt to discover what the meaning of the company for its customers and environment actually is. For example, Dutch bank ABN Amro used "The Bank" as a marketing slogan but found out that this was perceived as arrogant. It is now experimenting with a new concept to get to know the needs of their clients – "Bankshops" which include coffee corners. The basic idea for reconciliation of this dimension is this: through being responsive to client needs, develop the pull to push your products.

Stable continuity versus dynamic change

This dimension distinguishes between pursuing stable continuity versus looking for continuous, radical change. The business issue lies in how fast business models are supposed to change. Should a company continuously innovate to develop revolutionary products, disruptive technology, constantly seeking to exceed customer demands, or should it stick to its core, work on sustaining technology, and manage corporate transformation in steady stages? The dynamic change side of the dimension has been very much in favor over the past decade, but the risks of taking this to the extreme has been revealed in recent years. Many disruptive technologies fail. Enron gave up its stable business model of natural gas and pipelines to turn into a dynamic online energy trader. British chemical company ICI moved into specialty chemicals, but paid too much for a business it didn't know well enough. Dutch baby food producer Numico went into the vitamin business, with disastrous results because selling vitamin pills did not fit their traditional business model. The company had to sell its acquisitions in the vitamin business at a huge loss and is now trying to make a healthy profit in baby food again. British Cable & Wireless changed from a traditional telecommunications company to a company specializing in Internet Protocol services with disastrous results – in 2003, under a new CEO, it began a change program called "Back to Reality." Reconciliation occurs when companies realize that, paradoxically, you have to change if you want to remain the same, and pursue a stable continuity of core values if you want to experience continuous change. This is what Nokia did when it completely transformed its business into mobile telecommunications. It is also in line with Intel boss Andrew Grove's phrase "only the paranoid survive" (Grove, 1996): a business should be constantly prepared for the unplanned and unexpected. One way to do this is to try to predict and lead customer demand while continuing to develop sustaining technologies for the existing mainstream market, rather than forcing a disruptive technology into a market where it will not fit. Scenario planning is another way to reconcile this dilemma. Scenario planning is not so much about making projections of the future, but more about developing patterns of thinking to be able to estimate risks, thus combining change and stability. Scenario planning helped Shell to be prepared for the oil crisis in the 1980s, and Federal Credit Union (which was very dependent on Enron's trading business) when it turned out to be one of the few companies that had a scenario covering the possibility that Enron would go bankrupt.

Long-term, stakeholder orientation versus short-term, shareholder orientation

This dimension of corporate culture is about the extent to which the company focuses on short-term shareholder value versus long-term economic value for all stakeholders. The dilemma is between short-term profit and growth on the one hand and long-term survival on the other. As Arie de Geus has stated, in his book *The Living Company* (1997), the main reason for the short life expectancy of most companies is their focus on profits. Long term survival requires an ability to learn which is linked to the extent to which the company is integrated into its environment. Developing strong bonds with all stakeholders, including communities, enables a greater depth of learning.

Reconciliation on this dimension comes through taking corporate responsibility, creating sustainable value for all stakeholders. One way of realizing this is to link employee assessment and career advancement to contributions to sustainable growth. For instance, if a company suddenly switches production to another region, it should still show its responsibility in supporting the "old" local environment. An example of reconciling this dimension through corporate responsibility is the "business in the classroom project" undertaken by consultancy companies in the Netherlands to relieve a temporary shortage of schoolteachers. The project brought valuable teaching experience for consultants involved in the project, and short-term and long-term social and ethical credentials for the companies.

Assessing corporate cultures

Assessment of corporate cultures can be done in different ways. Generic questionnaires in which respondents are asked to evaluate how things work in their corporate culture give a quantitative assessment of that culture. The nine dimensions and the dilemmas associated with each one will manifest themselves in different ways in different industries, countries, and companies. Generic questionnaires and purely quantitative assessment have their limitations, though they serve well as a basis for discussion. If corporate culture assessment is to be used as the basis for corporate culture change programs or post merger/post acquisition corporate culture integration projects, corporate culture assessment cannot be done simply by administering a questionnaire. To really understand a corporate culture, you have to get under the surface or even immerse yourself in it. Analysis of company documents, interviews, storytelling, focus groups, observations, even participating in the company's activities is then necessary.

We will now look at ways to use the nine dimensions and the reconciling corporate culture concept in more detail.

Constructing a corporate culture profile by assessing the position of the corporate culture on each of the nine dimensions

It is still possible to use the more or less traditional way of assessing a corporate culture by using a questionnaire which asks the respondents about their level of agreement with a statement that evaluates the position on one particular dimension of corporate culture.

An example of such a question evaluating the position on the dimension of dynamic change versus stable continuity is to ask the respondents with which of the following two statements they agree most:

"In our company we value responding quickly to changing markets."

"In our company we value being stable, predictable, and following the plan of action."

This assessment leads to a corporate culture profile on nine dimensions, as shown in Figure 3.1.

The value of this type of assessment is that it is gives input on the reference point of a corporate culture, on "where it comes from." In combination with more qualitative assessment, it can help people understand the potential problems in any mergers and acquisitions processes.

Take, for example, the differences between investment and credit banks on the nine dimensions of corporate culture. At THT we have

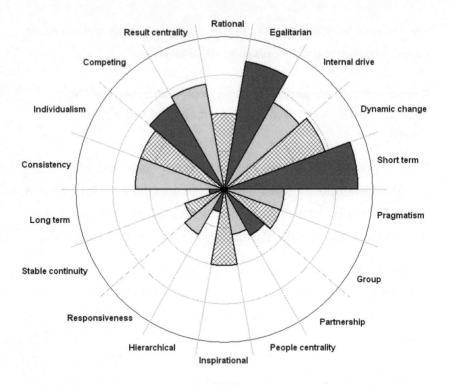

Figure 3.1 Corporate culture assessment on the nine corporate culture dimensions

worked with banks all over the world. By evaluating questionnaire results and examining input from managers and workshops, we have come up withe the following significant differences:

1. Credit banks tend to go for consistency whereas investment banks go for pragmatic solutions for particular client relationships.

2. At credit banks success is, to a large extent, rewarded in terms of social recognition by the group, but in investment banks success is rewarded by paying aggressively for individual performance in terms of income generated for the bank.

3. The relationship between credit banks can often be character-

ized by "friendly competition," but competition between investment banks is cut-throat in intensity.

4. In credit banks personal circumstances and loyalty still play a role (people centrality), but investment banks tend to have the "cut the crap mentality" typical for a high-pressure/high-stress/high-pay environment (result centrality).

5. Credit banks tend to have a rational, analytical, detached, unemotional atmosphere, while investment banks tend to have a more inspirational corporate culture, valuing imagination and finding new creative solutions – and may end up with a culture where showing emotions, shouting, and even swearing is acceptable. Imagination and finding new creative solutions tend to be more valued at investment banks, as well.

6. At credit banks career progression comes from slowly going through the hierarchical ranks; at investment banks people can advance more rapidly.

7. Credit banks have a moderate internal drive orientation because of relatively low tolerance for risk related to the nature of their business and the dependence on changing exchange and interest rates. Investment banks have a very high internal drive orientation and are more aggressive in pushing new products and services.

8. Credit banks tend to be more stable and traditional whereas investment banks need to be more dynamic in anticipating the rapidly changing markets and business environment.

9. Credit banks look at long-term survival while investment banks focus on short-term profit and shareholder value (see Figure 3.2).

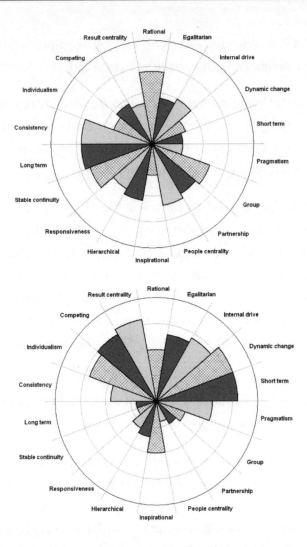

Figure 3.2 Typical corporate culture profile of credit bank (above) versus typical corporate culture profile of investment bank (below)

These differing corporate cultures have hindered the achievement of the synergies expected by financial analysts from mergers and acquisitions involving credit banks and investment banks. Examples include the merger between J.P. Morgan and Chase Manhattan Bank in 2000, the acquisition in 1998 of investment bank Robertson Stephens by Bank Boston (which was acquired one year later by

Fleet) and the acquisition of what was left of British investment bank Barings by the Dutch credit bank ING. Culture clashes related to each of the nine dimensions have had a bad effect on cooperation between the investment bank business and the rest of the company in all of these mergers and acquisitions.

This comparison between investment banks and credit banks is just a first order comparison. The nine dimension model also reveals clear differences between different investment banks, for example, the more rational, analytical, and individual performance-oriented Merril Lynch corporate culture versus the more team-oriented and imaginative culture of Goldman Sachs.

Constructing 2 x 2 matrices of corporate culture dimensions

We can also still use the model to construct 2x2 matrices by combining two corporate culture dimensions. These combinations can be useful for a first order analysis of specific aspects of corporate culture. Take, for instance, the two dimensions of our nine dimension model that are related to time orientation (Figure 3.3).

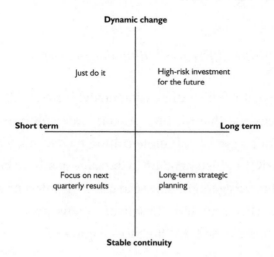

Figure 3.3   Corporate culture dimensions related to time orientation

Or take the two of the dimensions that are relevant for understanding corporate culture in terms of communication styles, conflict handling, and the meaning of work: rational versus inspirational and people centrality versus result centrality (Figure 3.4).

Figure 3.4 Corporate culture dimensions relevant for communication, conflict handling and work relationships

Corporate culture differences within one industry

An advantage of the nine dimension model is that it allows a focus on the dimensions that distinguish corporate cultures within one industry. While in most corporate culture models all start-up companies in the ICT industry end up in the same quadrant because they are pragmatic and egalitarian, we can use the result centrality versus people centrality and individualism versus group orientation dimensions to focus on the differences (Figure 3.5).

The result centrality/individualism quadrant fits the culture of the

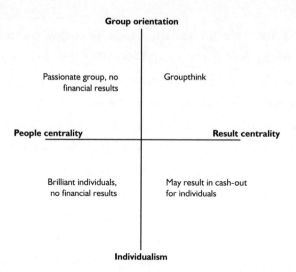

Figure 3.5   Corporate culture differences within the ICT industry

type of company that has a primary goal of preparing for an event such as an IPO or an acquisition by an established player. The focus in this type of company is, as mentioned before in Chapter 2, on quick and strong market presence and, for some individuals, on getting rich quickly. Internet startup Worldonline comes to mind, which immediately shows the downside of this corporate culture type: it risks destroying value instead of creating it.

The people centrality/group oriented quadrant fits the culture of a company created with the idea in mind of looking for others who shared the passion and founding a company with deeply held values and a strong culture – in order to make a difference, not just to make money. Steve Jobs' venture Next comes to mind, which illustrates the downside of this corporate culture type: lack of result orientation making it hard to survive in the long term.

The result centrality/group oriented quadrant fits the culture of the Japanese internet company Softbank. Softbank's founder Masayoshi Son had been an entrepreneur in the US before he started Softbank.

He realized that it would be harder to be an entrepreneur in Japan's business culture and that it would be difficult to attract employees because people preferred to work for the big companies. However, because he had to hire former truck drivers and other people without formal qualifications, he discovered that his employees were not just loyal but even devoted to the company. He tried to make use of this team spirit by giving teams their own balance sheets, so that they would feel the direct impact of their initiatives on the bottom line. The downside of this type of culture is that it easily turns into a "follow the leader" culture where nobody dares to challenge the leader of the group even when the risks are too high – which is the story of Softbank.

The quadrant of people centrality/individualism fits the corporate culture of Silicon Graphics in its early days, when it was described as a loose collection of argumentative, brilliant, headstrong engineers (Lewis, 2000), who were certainly going to use their creativity to develop wonderful technology but were not necessarily going to deliver financial results. Anarchy is probably the best word to describe the corporate culture of Silicon Graphics at the time, and the company went almost bankrupt before a task-oriented executive was hired to bring in more professionalism, hierarchy, and systems, and make the company less dependent on one or more individuals. In fact, all the ventures of Silicon Graphics' eccentric founder Jim Clark, including Netscape and Healtheon, shared this people oriented/individualism culture, leading to situations close to anarchy and the need for an outside professional manager to come to the rescue.

Although the example in Figure 3.5 shows that the nine dimension framework can help make corporate culture assessment more discriminating, it confirms that embracing a set of extreme value orientations is likely to lead to failure on the long run. Therefore we have to assess to what extent corporate cultures reconcile cultural differences.

ASSESSING THE EXTENT TO WHICH CORPORATE CULTURES RECONCILE DIFFERENT CULTURAL ORIENTATIONS

A first order assessment of the extent to which corporate cultures reconcile different value orientations can be obtained by a generic questionnaire. For instance, look at the five possible responses to the following question:

Which of the following statements best describes the type of jobs in your organization?

(a) *Jobs that are part of a team and the organization, where everyone works together without bothering about individual credit.*

(b) *Jobs that allow everyone to work independently and where credit is given for individual performance without dilution.*

(c) *Jobs where everyone works together in teams to help the organization, but where teams encourage, stimulate, reward, and celebrate individual contributions.*

(d) *Jobs which allow everyone to work independently for personal recognition, but where credit and acclaim come from the team and organization.*

(e) *Jobs which control both the excesses of the dominant individual and avoid too much conformity and groupthink.*

Each of the possible responses corresponds with a different way of dealing with the dilemma of individualism versus group orienta-

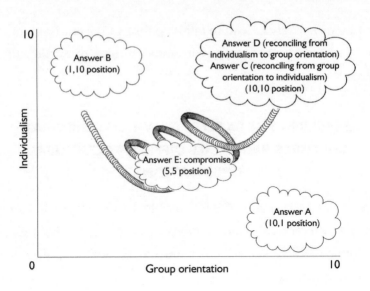

Figure 3.6 Assessment of the extent to which corporate cultures are reconciling cultures

tion, which are illustrated in Figure 3.6. Answer "a" points at a group-oriented culture; answer "b" points at an individualistic corporate culture. Answer "c" shows a culture that comes from the group-oriented side of the dimension, but which reconciles with individualism. Answer "d" illustrates a culture that comes from the individualistic side of the dimension, but reconciles it with group orientation, while answer "e" shows a compromise between individualism and group orientation.

Again, to make a full assessment of the extent to which a corporate culture reconciles, we need more than just a generic questionnaire. In our consulting practice we have been in the position to combine questionnaires with document analysis, web-based and in-depth face-to-face interviews, storytelling, observations, and other methods to get a more complete description of corporate cultures.

Silicon Valley corporate cultures

This has enabled us to position long-term successful Silicon Valley corporate cultures on a reconciliation chart, which helps in understanding why copying such cultures has turned out to be difficult. During the Silicon Valley hype in the 1990s these cultures were described as having a set of cultural value orientations that were exactly opposite to the cultural value orientations of companies with what was dubbed "traditional management" (Saxenian, 1994; James, 1998). Table 3.1 shows that these opposite value orientations correspond with the extremes on our nine corporate culture dimensions.

However, our work with Silicon Valley corporate cultures which have been succesful in the long term shows that the set of extreme cultural orientations in the second column of Table 3.1 does not represent them realistically. Successful Silicon Valley corporate cultures are characterized by continuous reconciliation of the fundamental corporate culture dilemmas shown in the third column of Table 3.1:

- Continuous learning from exceptions providing the information needed to take responsibility.
- Through shared vision, motivate to reach targets.
- Co-opetition.
- Through showing concern for employees, making them self-motivated entrepreneurs.
- Work is fun: inspiration through thorough analysis.
- Empowering employees through clear decision making structures.
- Through learning about customers needs, create markets for innovative products.
- Change being a way of life.
- Sustainable shareholder value.

Table 3.1 "Traditional management" and Silicon Valley cultures descibed as "ideal type" (adapted from Saxenian, 1994; James, 1998; Lewis, 2000), and corresponding corporate culture dimensions

Traditional Management	Silicon Valley Cultures described as "ideal type"	Corporate culture dimension
Management is systemic control	An informal, unconventional culture in which teams form their own rules and direction	Consistency versus pragmatism
People are motivated by fear for the consequences of not meeting their individual targets	People are motivated by loyalty to the higher purpose of the organization	Individualism versus group orientation
Business is a battlefield	Business is an ecosystem made up of organic partnerships formed to exploit market niches	Competing versus partnership orientation
Employees are resources	Self-fulfillment and learning are the essence of the corporation	Result centrality versus people centrality
Decisions are taken in an analytical way helped by computer systems. Work is separate from the rest of life	Intuition, creativity and passion are at the heart of decision making. Work is so enjoyable that your life is your work and you have your friends there.	Rational versus inspirational
Employees are like children	Managers see employees as colleagues, in charge of their own destiny	Hierarchical versus egalitarian
Markets need to be conquered	Quickly adapt to new market conditions	Internal drive versus responsiveness
Change is pain	Change is embracing opportunities for growth and the "new, new thing"	Stable continuity versus dynamic change
Companies are machines for profit	Companies are there for success of the community at large	Short-term shareholder versus long-term stakeholder orientation

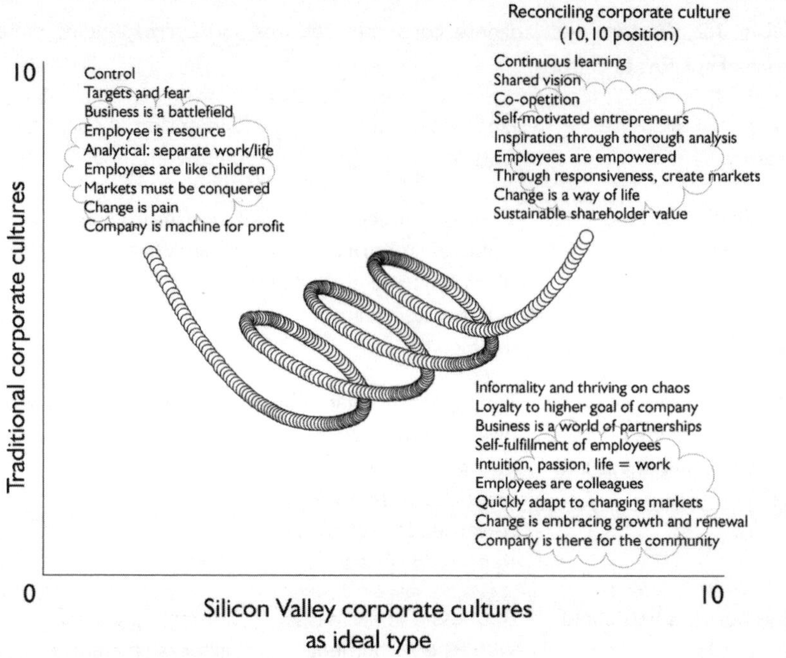
Reconciling corporate culture
(10,10 position)
Continuous learning
Shared vision
Co-opetition
Self-motivated entrepreneurs
Inspiration through thorough analysis
Employees are empowered
Through responsiveness, create markets
Change is a way of life
Sustainable shareholder value
10
Control
Targets and fear
Business is a battlefield
Employee is resource
Analytical: separate work/life
Employees are like children
Markets must be conquered
Change is pain
Company is machine for profit
Traditional corporate cultures
Informality and thriving on chaos
Loyalty to higher goal of company
Business is a world of partnerships
Self-fulfillment of employees
Intuition, passion, life = work
Employees are colleagues
Quickly adapt to changing markets
Change is embracing growth and renewal
Company is there for the community
0
10
Silicon Valley corporate cultures
as ideal type

Figure 3.7 Silicon Valley reconciling corporate cultures

The reconciliation is graphically represented in Figure 3.7.

Japanese corporate culture

We can also apply the nine dimensions of corporate culture and the concept of the reconciling corporate culture in order to understand what makes it so difficult for western companies to copy Japanese corporate cultures successfully. Business writers have tried to pin down Japanese corporate culture and western corporate cultures at opposite extremes of cultural value orientations. This made it easy to explain success and failure. And, superficially, the characteristics of Japanese corporate culture as described in the literature (Bratton, 1992; Campbell and Burton, 1994; Hayashi, 1988; March, 1992; Nonaka and Takeuchi, 1995; Johansson and Nonaka, 1996) can be

Table 3.2 Western and Japanese corporate cultures and corresponding dimensions of corporate culture

Western corporate culture	Japanese corporate culture	Dimension of corporate culture
Detailed procedures and systems	Control is based on personal authority (flexibility) and embedding in integrated teams (ambiguity)	Consistency versus pragmatism
People are motivated by rewards for their individual initiatives and performance	People are motivated by loyalty to the higher purpose of the organization and are rewarded for contributing to common goals	Individualism versus group orientation
Business is a battlefield	Business is in harmony with its environment	Competing versus partnership culture
Employees are resources, task oriented, impersonal	Mutual dependence, concern for employees including social life, family feeling	Result centrality versus people centrality
Explicit policies and communication	Idealistic philosophies	Rational versus inspirational
Democratic leadership	Paternalistic leadership	Egalitarian versus hierarchical
Technology push	Customer is king	Internal drive versus responsiveness
Discontinuous change, fast promotion, no job security	Continuous improvement, slow promotion, lifetime employment	Dynamic change versus stable continuity
Profit oriented – short-term results	Corporate philosophy focused on the common good – long time horizon	Short-term shareholder versus long-term stakeholder orientation

indeed be located at the other extreme of all nine dimensions of corporate culture, as is shown in Table 3.2.

The results of copying aspects of Japanese corporate cultures by western companies has, in many instances, not been satisfactory. The reason for this is that characterizing Japanese corporate cultures with the set of extreme value orientations, as in the second column of Table 3.2, does not acknowledge that there are many apparent contradictions in how Japanese management culture really works. In our work for Japanese companies and Western–Japanese joint ventures, we have encountered the following apparent contradictions, which turn out to be caused by the fact that many Japanese companies have reconciling corporate cultures:

- Although you often encounter flexibility and ambiguity in Japanese corporate cultures, for instance in the way that job descriptions are written (if they exist at all), you frequently also encounter careful documentation and precision, and clear rules and systems. Joseph Juran, the American founder of the systematic approach to Quality Management, was a hero among Japanese corporations way before his work was appreciated in the western world. It is important to understand that quality is defined by the user in Japan, not the producer. Assessment of quality starts with looking outside of the company, where particular situations lead to quality problems. This input is used for a systematic, company-wide approach to realize a quality culture. In Japanese corporate culture, consistency (systematic quality control) and pragmatism (flexible solutions for the user's quality problems) are reconciled.
- Loyalty and contributing to common goals are important aspects of Japanese corporate cultures, but you often encounter a lack of interpersonal trust, fights behind the scenes between

factions in the company, and interdepartmental conflict. If one can speak of harmony at all, this is realized by external coordination at a higher hierarchical level. In Japanese corporate culture taking initiatives by individual departments is stimulated through establishing loyalty and trust in a small group. This is then coordinated by the next level up the hierarchy.

- Although the Japanese business environment is in many ways cooperative and harmonious by nature – as is shown by nonadverserial relationships in the supply chain – there is fierce competition between Japanese companies in the market. The Japanese system stimulates competitiveness through co-operation: co-opetition.

- Instilling family feeling, caring for employees, and placing an emphasis on humanity and warmth are an integral part of Japanese corporate cultures, but Japanese managers can be very neutral and cold in other settings. Through putting people at the center, tough messages and a focus on results are made more acceptable.

- Vaguely formulated idealistic philosophies are part of many Japanese corporate cultures, but policies and plans are based on a process of carefully collecting detailed information. Through idealistic philosophies, people are inspired to pursue rational objectives.

- Paternalistic leadership is the dominant leadership style in Japanese corporate culture though this is combined with a consensus-style decision making process in which bottom-up participation in decision making is ensured. Moreover, leaders often combine their high status with a humble and egalitarian appearance, for instance by wearing company uniforms in the workplace. Through bottom-up collecting of information, decisiveness by hierarchical leadership is accepted.

- Although the "customer is king" attitude is definitely present in Japanese corporate cultures, Japanese companies manage to push innovative products onto the market with great success as well. Telecommunications company DoCoMo's success in bringing third generation, wide band CDMA mobile phone service ("I-mode") to the market was due to a management that listened carefully to what the market was telling them, so that they could develop a service tailored to what customers wanted. DoCoMo kept tight control over selecting content suppliers and handset manufacturers (push) but developed an open system, so that it was easy for outside content providers to develop content for I-mode (pull). This "pushing the pull" culture is characteristic of Japanese corporate cultures.

- Continuous, step-by-step improvement is an essential part of Japanese corporate culture, but very rapid change occurs as well. Rapid change is acceptable in Japanese corporate cultures when there is a consensus that it is the right thing to do, based on long-term vision and qualitative planning. Japanese companies sometimes embark on large-scale projects that would normally have been considered too risky for cultures which favor detailed planning . The huge investment in the American entertainment industry by Sony is a case in point. The speed with which Japan introduced the bullet train is another example of the acceptance of rapid change. Remember that "just in time" management, the ultimate reconciliation between step-by-step planning and timing change, was invented within a Japanese corporate culture context.

- Long-term orientation seems to be dominant in Japanese corporate cultures, as is shown by patience, long-term vision, and willingness to take short-term losses and invest in the future. However, short-term behavior is also there, such as was seen

YEOVIL COLLEGE
LIBRARY

in the speculative behavior on the Japanese market in the 1980s. Pursuing short-term goals can become dominant in Japanese corporate cultures when there is a need to catch up with others or show immediate profits. For instance, when Matshushita bought American entertainment company MCA including Universal Studios in 1990, this was in fact a short-term reaction to catch up with Sony, which had bought Columbia Pictures in 1989. Matshushita sold MCA in 1995. Here's another example – when a Japanese food company started its European operations, the reports of sales results included products which had been shipped to supermarkets, but which had been returned because they hadn't sold before the expiry date. Reporting a high turnover to motivate employees in the short term was considered to be more important than long-term consistency in sales results.

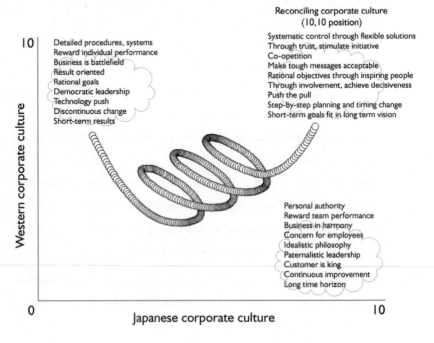

Figure 3.8 Japanese corporate cultures as reconciling cultures

The analysis of these apparent contradictions shows that successful Japanese companies continuously reconcile "traditional Japanese" corporate culture values with western corporate culture values (Figure 3.8).

This analysis of Japanese corporate cultures as reconciling corporate cultures is a special case of the impact of globalization on corporate culture as discussed in Chapter 1 – learning from local cultural values to improve a global corporate culture. This brings us to the topic of understanding the impact of national cultures on corporate culture values.

CHAPTER 4

Corporate culture:
the international perspective

What is more important for understanding the impact of culture on cooperation in international business, corporate culture or national culture? Different views on this issue lead to an ongoing debate involving managers, consultants, and academics.

In our view, it is not a matter of either/or. The reality is that the patterns of national culture in the place where a company has its roots have so much influence on company culture that the national cultural background needs to be understood in order to understand the workings of its corporate culture in an international context. As discussed in Chapter 2, national cultures vary substantially on their relative preferences for the four corporate cultures shown in Figure 2.1, which means that the impact of national culture cannot be neglected. However, it is a serious mistake to assume that the culture preferred in the domestic HQ of an international company will work throughout the world. Globalization imposes seemingly conflicting demands on companies: combining global effectiveness in production, distribution, and service; exploitation of know-how on a worldwide scale; integrating local managers into the global management infrastructure, and adapting to local circumstances and needs. The solution lies in not just finding a balance between global corporate culture and the necessary adaptation to local management practices, the culture of local employees, and to local market situations. A reconciled solution requires learning from local cultures on a continuous basis in order to improve the global effectiveness of the corporate culture.

Part of this process is internationalization of management boards, which is proceeding rapidly. For instance, 19 out of the 21 largest companies listed on the Dutch stock market have at least one non-Dutch board member.

This does not mean that the ideal global company is "culture free," that is, without clearly discernable roots in national culture. ABB, the global engineering giant, is a case in point. After the merger between Swedish Asea and Swiss Brown Boveri in 1987, a new ABB "virtual headquarters" was established in Zurich, staffed by only 100 people. ABB's first CEO, Percy Barnevik, proudly said that ABB was a company with no natural center, a company not with one home but with many homes, and that its headquarters might as well be on board a Boeing 747. At the time, ABB was heralded as the example for the future, the company that had gone the furthest down the multicultural route, with four nationalities represented in ABB's board of eight directors, five nationalities on the executive committee, and English as the corporate language (Economist, 1994). At the end of the 1990s ABB started a steep downfall, partly caused by difficult market conditions and legal claims but also partly by weak management due to the loss of ABB's identity and roots, for which nothing else had been substituted. ABB had not been on a multicultural route, it had been going down a culture-free one.

We can see ample proof that home-country culture remains important for the creation of company-specific competitive advantage, which then needs to be translated into international competitiveness. Those companies that can assimilate diversity in a positive way have a good chance of succeeding globally, but they do need to address a number of conflicting values, as is illustrated in Figure 4.1.

GLOBALIZING COMPANIES

Let's look at some globalizing companies with their roots in different cultures, to assess how they reconcile their national cultural roots with a global corporate culture.

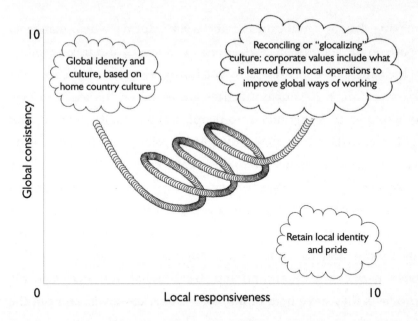

Figure 4.1 Corporate culture in a global context – the dilemma of global consistency versus local responsiveness

Sweden: The IKEA way

IKEA, the Swedish furniture retailer, profiles itself very much as a Swedish company. All outlets are painted in the same colours, the blue and yellow of the Swedish flag, and they even sell Swedish food. It is a values-driven company with a clear philosophy formulated by founder and long-term CEO, Ingvar Kamprad: "We shall offer a wide range of home furnishing items of good design and function, at prices so low that the majority of people can afford to buy them" (Torekull, 1998). This philosophy reflects Swedish values, such as egalitarianism and functionality, simplicity and down-to-earthness. IKEA's philosophy and values are translated into management practices, products, and selling concepts.

The company has a flat organization, practices consensus decision making, has an "anti-bureaucratic week" during which managers work on the shop floor, casual dress at all levels, and travel policies which include coach-class travel for everyone and cheap hotel rooms. Human Resource practices are based on the idea "to give down-to-earth, straightforward people the possibility to grow, both as individuals and in their professional roles," and include hiring young people with similar values in any culture. IKEA's products are designed to be simple, "young at heart," and durable. Suppliers are seen as partners who work together with IKEA to reduce costs. The number of sales staff is kept at a minimum level. Furniture, showroom, and warehouse are combined in one building, so that customers can walk around and decide what they like, load the products they have bought into their cars themselves, and put the furniture together at home. Shopping becomes a day out, and going with the whole family is stimulated by facilities for children, including a cheap children's menu in the restaurant.

After Ingvar Kamprad withdrew as CEO in 1986, his successor was Anders Moberg. Like Kamprad, he was a farmer's son; he even came from the same region and shared the same values. These values can still be recognized in IKEA's corporate culture as described above: consistency (by being clear on vision and values, not by putting directives on paper), individual initiative, partnership orientation, people centrality, rationality, egalitarianism and an open, informal communication climate, responsiveness to customer's needs, stable continuity, and long-term orientation. These are all at the heart of IKEA's corporate culture.

IKEA has gone through a rapid internationalization process, and is now active all over Europe, in North America, and in some parts of East Asia including Hong Kong, Singapore, and Malaysia. IKEA's corporate culture has helped to keep the company focused during globalization, but it has turned out to be difficult to explain the egalitarian spirit, people centrality, and long-term orientation in other cultures. In Germany, informal ways of addressing bosses, taking individual initiative, and not recognizing status related to position in the hierarchy were problems that had to be overcome (Germany is a less individualistic and more hierarchical culture). In Southern Europe, the need was felt for more clarity about responsibilities at different hierarchical levels, and for knowing the possibility of being promoted (a more hierarchical culture). In the US some local managers left the company because they could not get used to a corporate culture that was seen as too rational without room for showing emotions, that did not offer compensation linked to individual performance, did not tolerate competitive behavior, and that gave long-term directions, but not enough short-term instruction (the US is more individualistic, competing, and short-term oriented). IKEA's

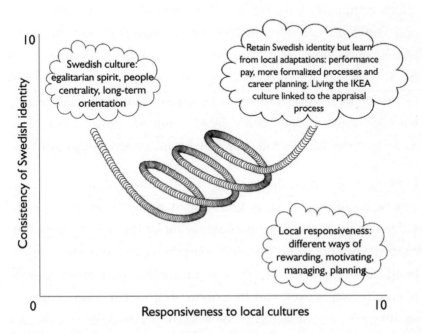

Figure 4.2 IKEA's corporate culture in a global context

reaction to these encounters with different value orientations has been not to give up its Swedish identity, but to start a process of reconciliation (Figure 4.2): put more clear responsibilities on paper, introduce more formal performance reviews, link compensation more to performance, introduce development programs and career planning, and – most important of all – make living the IKEA corporate culture values part of the appraisal process.

The Netherlands: transatlantic mishaps

It seems to be a general opinion among business analysts that out of all continental European business cultures, Dutch business culture comes closest to that of Anglo-Saxon businesses. Examples of successful British–Dutch cooperations such as Unilever and Shell, and the fact that the Netherlands is the biggest foreign investor in the US, are used to support this statement. However, over the past decade Dutch companies have faced major problems in Dutch–American and Dutch–British cooperation. The existence of several major Dutch companies was threatened because of failed acquisitions in the US: retailer Ahold, food company Numico and IT companies Getronics and Baan Company, to name just a few. Philips Electronics has been active in the US for decades, but has never managed to make its American operations profitable on a sustainable basis.

Looking at our nine dimensions of corporate culture, Dutch and American cultures do indeed have many things in common – individualism, for instance – but there are major differences as well. In contrast with the result-oriented, competitive and short-term orientated American culture, Dutch culture is much more people oriented, cooperative and long term. The Dutch combination of egalitarianism, people orientation, and cooperativeness leads to corporate cultures with the decentralized responsibility of subsidiaries.

Numico and Getronics found out that they could not motivate the former owners and managers of their acquired companies in the US; the enormous losses threatened their very survival.

At Ahold the consequences were even worse. Ahold was originally a family-owned and managed company, and its market leadership in the Netherlands was due to its strong identity as a Dutch company and to the loyalty of clients, customers, and shareholders. When Ahold's internationalization process rapidly gathered speed in the 1990s, it did not actually have enough management capacity to integrate acquisitions in different parts of the world. In combination with the Dutch tendency to decentralize responsibility, this led to lack of control in overseas subsidiaries, especially in the US. Ahold had bought different supermarket chains in the US, and in the end they all adopted the culture of the most powerful of these chains, Stop & Shop, instead of a global Ahold culture. Ahold lost its Dutch identity in the internationalization process, and this also had an impact on its board. CEO van der Hoeven (although a Dutch national) started to act more and more as an American-style celebrity CEO. While Dutch companies normally cherish a consensus-based decision making process in their boards, van der Hoeven took a very dominant position. Ahold became a "follow the leader" culture, without the checks and balances normally present in the Dutch consensus system.

The company participated in the frantic environment of the second half of the 90s, making more and more acquisitions and taking more risks than fitted its original corporate culture. The acquisition of US Foodservice, a company in a business outside Ahold's core retail business, was an example of this. Ahold discovered too late that American business culture was very different from its traditional corporate culture, and that they should have taken more time to diffuse their own corporate values. They found out that, in American culture, implementing pay for individual performance without proper control might lead to managers focusing on reaching the targets for their bonuses without working in the interests of the company as a whole. They also found out that very aggressive marketing techniques were acceptable in an American business environment, even though they did not fit with Ahold's culture. American short-term orientation showed up in a lack of investment in product innovation, contrary to Ahold's long-term oriented culture.

When these problems were discovered, former IKEA CEO Anders Moberg, who had continued his career at US company Home Depot, had to be brought in to save Ahold. The damage had been done. Moberg's remuneration package included performance incentives that may have been acceptable in an American business environment, but were not in the more egalitarian Dutch environment. The problems in international operations even caused a loss of loyalty among Ahold's Dutch customers.

Ahold was forced to take far-reaching measures to restore confidence and trust among customers and shareholders. Chairman of the supervisory board Henny de Ruiter resigned, CEO Moberg's remuneration package was considerably changed (reducing his basic salary and making bonuses more dependent on performance) in order to make it more acceptable, and Ahold significantly lowered the prices in its Albert Heijn stores in the Netherlands in order to tempt customers back – at the expense of creating a price war with other food retailers. The company seems to be out of the immediate danger zone, but its reputation and global aspirations have been severely affected.

The Ahold case shows the risk of believing that when there are great

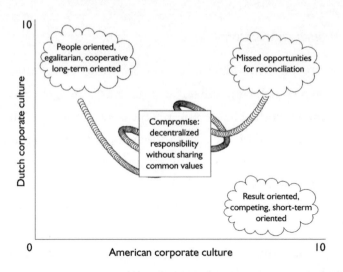

Figure 4.3 US acquisitions of Dutch companies – missed opportunities for reconciliation

opportunities for business synergies one can afford to ignore the cultural issues. As a consequence, Ahold failed to explore possibilities for reconciliation, such as making people responsible for a part of the synergy in, for instance, distribution, purchasing, administration, and corporate culture (Figure 4.3).

On a positive note, the Ahold case has influenced how Dutch CEOs think about the impact of corporate culture differences in an international context. The CEO of the Dutch bank ABN Amro, Rijkman Groenink, used to be known as an Americanized CEO, a fervent supporter of American business culture. However, after the Ahold debacle he commented that Americans don't want to be dominated by Dutch bosses and might even try to become dominant themselves, as in a reverse takeover. He added that although it was conceivable to have an American as the CEO of a company like ABN Amro, that individual should have the capacity to be a carrier of the company culture and therefore be able to represent the more open, egalitarian, consensus-based, flexible European business culture.

Suez: French connections

Remarkably, the two global leaders in the water distribution business are two French companies, Suez (formerly Suez Lyonnaise des Eaux) and Vivendi. This is not a coincidence. Their international approach was based on the French model of outsourcing public services to a private company (Prud'homme and Trompenaars, 2001). Typical of this approach was the 25–30 year contract for the building, operating, and management of water distribution. Suez is now a global player in the business of providing utility systems and infrastructure, including water, energy, and waste management. The group's business model is significantly based on its successful, long-lasting history in water distribution.

We can recognize many French cultural characteristics present in Suez' corporate culture when it started its globalization process:

- An informal, pragmatic approach based on strong local relationships. Each contract is different and adapted to suit local history and culture. Suez understands local situations and the need for local autonomy because of unique political and personal relationships with municipalities and governments, and cooperation with many former local monopolies. Here we can recognize the corporate culture values of pragmatism and partnership – "partnership" is actually one of Suez' core values.
- A group spirit based on sharing and exchanging knowledge in a personal network of French expatriates. This clearly shows the group orientation and people centrality corporate culture orientations.
- Strong charismatic leadership at the corporate center and diplomatic skills in networking with governments around the world. We can discern the corporate culture orientations of inspirational and hierarchical here.

- Strength in dealing with endemic uncertainties. Both the water and energy business are involved in codeveloping regions that are politically instable. The corporate culture orientation of internal drive can be seen clearly here.

- Combining entrepreneurial spirit with long-term horizons in the provision of infrastructure: you cannot load a network of water pipes or a power plant on to your back and leave a country. Dynamic change and long-term orientation are the cultural values which can be seen clearly here.

These corporate culture values fit the French corporate culture preferences: pragmatism, group orientation, partnership orientation, people centrality, inspirational, hierarchical, internal drive, dynamic change, and long-term orientation. Suez' CEO Gérard Mestrallet recognized, when he was appointed in 1997, that further globalization would reveal the weaknesses of the company's corporate culture. He realized that Suez was not a global company nor a transnational, but a French company with an international operation. He realized that Suez had to address its weaknesses without losing its strengths, had to become global through its strengths in localization. The weaknesses were the mirror sides of its strengths: weakness in formal planning and decision making, lack of profit orientation, giving too much autonomy to local operations, and exercising insufficient formal control. Moreover, since national sensibilities matter when you try to gain control of local operations, strong leadership from the center had the risk of being seen as seen as "French hauteur." When we look at Suez' current corporate culture, as reflected in its core values, we see that Suez fits the reconciling corporate culture concept, as shown in Figure 4.4.

Suez' corporate value of global ethical conduct balances the informal approach based on strong local relationships. The corporate

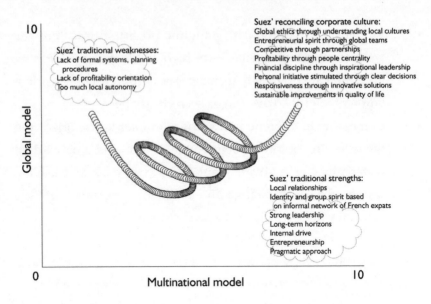

Figure 4.4 Development of Suez' corporate culture in a global context

value of team spirit ensures that entrepreneurial spirit is rooted in working in global teams. The corporate value of partnership ensures that Suez remains competitive through partnerships with local authorities, business associates, local investors, international institutions, non-governmental organizations, and end users. Value creation as a corporate value ensures that profitability is an integral part of Suez' corporate culture, so that people centrality and result centrality are balanced. Value creation also stresses the need for financial discipline – balancing the rational and inspirational culture orientations. The corporate value of professionalism ensures that personal initiative is stimulated. Professionalism also stands for innovative solutions, ensuring responsiveness to clients' needs – such as providing integrated water, energy, and waste services. The corporate value of respect for the environment involves seeking the creation of sustainable improvements in quality of life, ensuring both stable continuity and a balance between short-term and long-term orientation.

It is clear that Suez, coming from the model of the French multinational, with traditional strengths in a decentralized organization with informal ways of working, is well on its way to shaping a transnational organization. This is based on a corporate culture reconciling French strengths, corresponding with the multinational model, and cultural orientations, corresponding with the global model (Figure 4.4).

The choices made by Suez are by no means self-evident or easy. Mestrallet could have easily followed the advice of consultants to transform his company into an Enron-like trader. However, Mestrallet, a graduate of French elite educational institutes the Grand Ecole Polytechnique and the Ecole Nationale d'Administration, has never imitated American ways. Now compare Suez with Vivendi, that other French global leader in the same industry. Vivendi was also a utilities company rooted in the Paris establishment. However under Jean-Marie Messier, a former investment banker, the American entertainment company Universal was acquired and Vivendi Universal became one of the world's largest media and communications companies. Messier acted as a fervent supporter of American business culture and spent most of his time in New York presenting himself as an Anglo-Saxon-style boss. Vivendi Universal became a cultural and commercial disaster, leading to the disgrace of Messier and perhaps to the conviction that French business should not forget its cultural roots.

Nokia: connecting Finnish values

Part of Nokia's early success in the mobile telephone business was reportedly due to the fact that its brand name was initially seen as Japanese (Steinbock, 2001), instead of one from a small Nordic country without an international reputation in electronics or telecommunications. However most people now recognize Nokia as "the legend from Finland," and admire it for turning itself from a small conglomerate into a leading mobile phone manufacturer. Nokia executives describe the company as an international company with a Finnish soul, and one that intends to remain true to its roots while becoming the global leader in mobile telecommunications.

That Finnish soul seems to have been essential in creating and maintaining Nokia's sharp competitive edge. The foundation of Nokia's culture is the Nokia Way (www.nokia.com), a combination of values, competencies, and operational mode and processes. We can see many elements that can be traced back to the roots of Finnish culture in the Nokia Way. Part of this Nokia Way is believing in a flat, networked organizational structure, in speed and flexibility in decision making, in nurturing discussion and openness, in encouraging entrepreneurialism, innovation, risk taking, teamwork, and accountability, as well as in uncompromising integrity and responsible management. Hierarchy in the organization is avoided as much as possible and employees are not judged by their titles. Nokia has been called the least hierarchical of the big companies in the world because of its informal and open culture. Nokia's non-Finnish employees describe their Finnish colleagues as very straightforward people who only talk when they need to talk, don't show off, don't try to impress others with their wealth, and who in general have a no-nonsense attitude: get the job done. The lack of hierarchy and the open communication explain the unusual lack of interdepartmental rivalry at Nokia, for example between marketing and engineers. It helps in building the trust necessary in order to come to quick decisions. Openness for diverging initiatives also explains the transformation from a small conglomerate to a company focusing on mobile technology.

Nokia's values are customer satisfaction, respect for the individual, achievement, and continuous learning. The customer satisfaction value reflects the fact that Nokia respects and cares for its customers, working in partnership with them to satisfy their needs. The value of respect for the individual shows that Nokia gives a great deal of responsibility and freedom to individuals and encourages open and frank communication. The value of achievement reflects the fact that Nokia empowers employees to set their own clear goals, and gives them the tools to reach them. The continuous learning value demonstrates that everyone at Nokia is entitled to develop themselves, to be entrepreneurial and innovative, to adapt to new situations, and to take risks. It also encourages a humble attitude and finding ways to improve individual performance. Nokia executives often use the Finnish word *nöyryyss* to explain their culture. It means humility in combination with quiet self-assurance: take pride in the past but don't project it into the future. CEO Jorma Ollila is the personification of this culture in leadership. Clearly, Nokia's corporate culture has its roots in cultural orientations that correspond with Finnish values: consistency, individualism (valuing individual freedom and initiative), partnership orientation, people centrality, a rational, no-nonsense attitude, egalitarianism, internal drive, openness for other perspectives and change, and a long-term orientation.

However, the Nokia Way also shows how that Nokia managed to create a reconciling corporate culture on the basis of these roots:

- Through consistency (strict financial controls and uncompromising integrity) it can afford free and flexible organizational characteristics.

- Through giving individual freedom and encouraging open communication, it stimulates sharing information in team efforts.

- Through building partnerships, it gains competitive edge: in mobile telephony, it is content that makes products successful, which Nokia realizes through its partnerships.

- Through giving employees all the information they need and empowering them to set their own goals, it obtains their personal commitment to stretched targets.

- Through egalitarianism and listening to everybody's input, it builds the trust needed to get commitment to quick decisions.

- Through a no-nonsense, straightforward attitude, it builds warm relationships.

- Through humbleness, it ensures that self-assurance and internal drive are not seen as arrogance.

- Through lifelong learning, it encourages people to stay at the forefront of technological development – so that they embrace

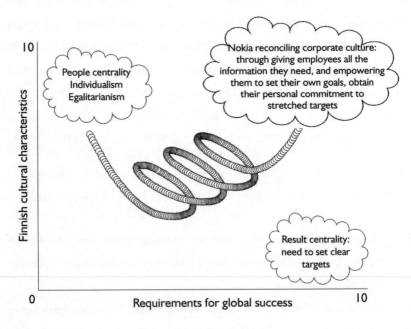

Figure 4.5 Nokia's corporate culture in a global context - reconciling people centrality and result centrality

dynamic change, entrepreneurship, and a culture of innovation.

- Through an inspiring long-term vision of becoming the global leader in mobile communications, it creates short-term shareholder value.

Nokia is another example of a company that globalizes successfully by connecting the values that lie at the heart of its corporate culture with the value orientations at the other extreme of the cultural dimensions, as shown in Figure 4.5.

American corporate cultures: you're either with us or against us

"Mainstream" American corporate cultures tend to value the corporate culture orientations of consistency, individualism, competing, result centrality, rational, egalitarian, internal drive, dynamic change, and short-term orientation. The combination of consistency, competing, and internal drive runs the risk of leading to a corporate culture characterized by a dominating attitude and a lack of willingness to reconcile. This is the problem that many American companies face.

Companies such as McDonald's globalize a successful formula, but run into problems when local competitors copy the formula and adapt it to local situations, local needs, or local taste. Even McDonald's faces the need to adapt to local cultures because of resistance to American dominance in France, the competition of local hamburger chains selling "rice burgers" in Asia, etc. Similarly, the seemingly unbeatable formula of retailer Wal-Mart has encountered problems in its globalization process because it is seen as too dominant. The formula of standardization, competitiveness, and result orientation gives low prices for customers, but it also results in low wages for employees, in reduced variety in product lines, and in more dependence on specific suppliers. It is too early to tell whether Wal-Mart's globalization effort will succeed, but some problems can be foreseen when it does not adapt its corporate culture. Wal-Mart began operations in Germany in 1997, but is still not profitable there. Germany favors stable continuity and long-term orientation – one consequence for retailers is that shops are not allowed to sell products below cost, while attracting customers by selling milk and bread below cost price is a strategy that Wal-Mart uses in the US. Germany's more people-oriented culture results in a much stronger position of the unions, and labor laws which ensure higher job security; Wal-Mart discourages employees from joining unions at all and has already had conflicts in Germany about this issue.

The risk of mainstream American corporate culture is that it comes across in globalization as "they come over here to explain to us what is wrong about our local way of doing things" – a complaint we have heard about American companies in many different industries, including industrial companies and investment banks. A willingness and ability to shape a reconciling corporate culture would help American companies be more successful in their globalization processes. Let's look at an American company that is a global leader in its industry, and which took an approach to globalization showing a willingness to reconcile its corporate culture based on the experiences in its investments abroad.

Applied Materials: total solutions

Applied Materials, the Silicon Valley-based global leader in equipment for semiconductor manufacturing, recognized in an early stage of its internationalization that globalization and localization (taking into account the special features and needs of each marketplace) needed to go hand in hand. One of Applied Materials' philosophies is always to go into a market early, because that forces them to learn from different local business environments. Applied Materials started a wholly-owned subsidiary in Japan in 1981, and many of the things that the company learned from competing in Japan are now applied globally (Morgan and Morgan, 1991; Trompenaars, Prud'homme, Park and Hampden-Turner, 2001). Here are some examples, looking at the Japanese situation and illustrating the reconciliations that Applied Materials have made.

The Japanese notion that human relations are the foundation of business. During the Japanese recession of 1985–6, instead of downsizing its Japanese operations Applied Materials assigned Japanese employees to other areas around the globe where their skills could be best utilized. Result centrality was reconciled with people centrality.

The Japanese notion of the customer is god, which is more extreme than the western equivalent of the customer is always right. Customers in Japan have high demands for service, quality, and delivery times. Applied Materials has incorporated into its corporate culture what has been learnt from Japanese ideas about the customer–supplier relationship: Service must precede all products, regardless of how advanced and unique they are. Internal drive was reconciled with responsiveness. Applied Materials even practiced this reconciliation in the decision about the succession of its long-term CEO Jim Morgan in 2003. It chose a former top executive from Intel, one of Applied's most important customers. The idea is that this move will help Applied to become even more responsive to what chipmakers want and expect, in order to compete better.

The Japanese concept anshin *(trust from the heart) used to describe the type of relationship with business partners.* Suppliers are loyal to their customers in Japan and in return they receive loyalty back. The relationship is an ongoing process of problem solving and opportunity creation. Applied Materials learned how to become a trusted preferred supplier by giving exceptionally good support, and then used this as a model throughout the world to build relationships with customers and to improve relationships with its own suppliers. Part of this is the notion that it is the customer's responsibility to help the supplier achieve excellence. "Practicing mutual trust" was made a core value at Applied Materials. Competing was reconciled with partnership orientation.

One of the main problems for foreign companies in Japan is attracting top people. Applied Materials' creative solution has been to make use of the Japanese fascination with leadership. Applied Materials used the charisma of its Japanese subsidiary's CEO to make it possible for them to hire top people. Rational was reconciled with inspirational.

The need to build a unique regional organization structure which promotes close interaction with customers. Being close to the customer enables Applied Materials to address their needs and continuously improve products, services, and customer satisfaction. By putting customers' business results first, customers share their advanced ideas with Applied Materials which then transforms them into products that consistently meet customer needs. For instance, when Applied Materials Korea grew rapidly with its Korean customers, and when Korean companies such as Samsung started to invest in the US, Applied Materials Korea established offices near Samsung's sites in order to deliver constant support to that customer's overseas investment projects. This unique regional organization ensured a customer interface centered around service, trust, and loyalty, rather than focusing on complete control from headquarters. It helps Applied Materials in offering customized combinations of modular solutions. Consistency was reconciled with pragmatism.

Fitting individuals into larger teams. Applied Materials found out, during its internationalization process, that the complementarity of individuals with diverse backgrounds is of the utmost importance in making teams effective. For Applied Materials it was a major issue in their globalization strategy to have a truly international team. More than 25 nationalities are now represented in its top 50 management team.

The need for long-term commitment. Applied Materials has earned a reputation in the Asian countries where it is active as a loyal, committed supplier, which hangs on in there in both good and bad times. Jim Morgan has described the essence of Applied Materials as "nothing in the world can take the place of persistence" (Newsweek, 2002). This has helped in overcoming the fear of non-commitment by foreign companies that exists in many Asian countries. For instance, when business slowed down in Korea during the monetary crisis in 1998, Applied Materials increased the budget for training and development, stressing the need for continuous learning. Short-term orientation was reconciled with long-term orientation. Applied Materials learned from this that a downturn is a good time to make sure that you have new technologies, processes, and management systems in place – which it used during the technology downturn in 2001.

The need to have shared values. Applied Materials is in one of the fastest moving industries at present and realized that, paradoxically, in order for its people to deal with the accelerating pace of change and the diversity of the partners in its business it needed to learn how to focus on the values it shared. Practicing effectively within the framework of the corporate values was made part of the reward criteria. Dynamic change was reconciled with stable continuity.

The need to be both collaborative and decisive. In the Japanese system, as much information as possible is gathered about a particular issue

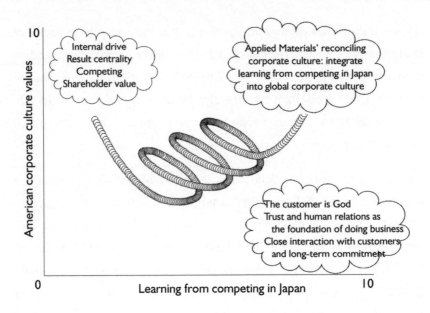

Figure 4.6 Applied Materials' corporate culture – integrating local learnings in a global context

and all viewpoints are considered in order to come to the right decision. But once the decision is made, the company moves as one. Applied Materials has utilized this combination of collaboration and decisiveness by continuously empowering local management, listening to viewpoints from around the world to come to those right decisions, and, once the decisions have been taken, bringing all energies and abilities together to move as a unit. Egalitarian and hierarchical were reconciled.

Applied Materials' openness to a free flow of ideas and its ability to deal with dilemmas and paradoxes have made it possible to integrate local learnings into its global corporate culture (Figure 4.6). Applied Materials shows that an American company can become the unchallenged global leader in its industry by creating such a reconciling corporate culture.

Acer

The Taiwanese company Acer is arguably the most globalized company which has its roots in Chinese culture. When Acer started its globalization process in the 1980s, its corporate culture was very much based on the traditional strengths of Taiwanese business culture (Prud'homme, 2001), in which we recognize extreme orientations on the nine dimensions of corporate culture as detailed below:

- Pragmatism and adaptability to the needs of customers and management practices based on highly personal and particular relationships between employers and employees. Flexibility has been an essential Taiwanese survival characteristic for centuries. There are no standardized rules for management practices in Confucianism, and Taiwan's economy is mainly based on small- and medium-sized enterprises where management can easily work without standardized rules.

- Group orientation. Acer's philosophy in its first years was "Creating the Dragon Dream." The idea was to motivate Acer's (at this stage almost exclusively ethnic Chinese) staff by the dream of creating what was to become the first multinational Chinese firm. Acer also used the term "commoner's culture" to emphasize a focus on low cost, frugality, and discipline.

- Partnership orientation. Acer's growth was initially based on its partnerships in OEM (original equipment manufacturer) agreements, that is, manufacturing to another firm's specifications and with its products marketed by that firm under the firm's brand names. Acer launched its own brand only in 1986. When Acer started to globalize it formed joint ventures with local partners whenever possible. Acer was a pioneer in building global technology partnerships with TI, IBM, etc. In forming these partnerships, Acer made use of its strength of not being afraid to lose control. As CEO Stan Shih once said: "I would rather lose control of the company to make money instead of tightening control and losing money" (Shih, 1996).

- People centrality. Acer's globalization was based on a close relationship network of Taiwanese managers and paternalistic caring.

- Inspirational, based on the charismatic leadership of long term CEO Stan Shih.

- Hierarchical. The term "shi-fu" (literally meaning teacher-father) used by employees to refer to superiors reflects the status associated with hierarchical position.

- Responsiveness. The focus on OEM contracts and external markets in Acer's first stages of development reinforced a culture of responsiveness to customer needs.

- Dynamic change and short-term orientation. The speed of change within the information technology industry played right into the hands of a company like Acer, where people were used to a dynamic time orientation: working in short bursts, making ad hoc decisions and quickly changing direction. Being a quick follower of competition and "cloning" their competitor's products instead of focusing on its own formal product planning was key to Acer's early success.

This corporate culture was less effective when Acer started to become a global company with many western employees. Having few rules and procedures and many exceptions became a problem when the company started to work with western employees who expected job descriptions, personnel manuals, and standard criteria for promotions. Local (individualistic-oriented) staff working for

Acer in the West had problems in coping with the expected loyalty to the company (such as expectations about willingness to work overtime) and also experienced a lack of trust between an "in-group" of expatriate managers versus an "out-group" of local staff. Acer's sober, low-cost culture with a focus on functionality and frugality was experienced by western employees as inhumane. Speed was an important source of competitive advantage, but for western staff the ad hoc decision-making culture was very confusing. They were used to more stability; Acer's management was even accused of dashing too fast. The perception of Acer's western staff was that the Taiwanese management had no long-term strategy and just followed developments in the market with a "we sell everything" mentality.

After a brief interval during which Acer's corporate culture was in danger of being eroded, due to a flood of new people and complacency because of its early success, the company became a global player by developing its own strategy, sometimes called the "fourth way of globalization," from 1992 onward. An analysis of its globalization strategy shows that it restored its corporate culture by reconciling aspects of traditional Chinese business culture with aspects of western business culture on all nine dimensions. Let's look at those in detail.

Reconciling consistency and pragmatism. Acer's global brand, local touch strategy. Coming from a culture that values pragmatic adaptation to the local environment, making Acer known as a global brand name with a good reputation has forced its corporate culture to incorporate more consistency – such as setting standard trademarks, channel structures, structured market research and sales policies, and consistent customer service.

Reconciling individualism and group orientation. Coming from a culture that believes in commitment and loyalty to group goals, Acer has introduced a stock ownership program to instill the loyalty of individuals.

Reconciling competing and partnership. Acer designed a "client–server" structure which allows each business to become an independent and separately operating client entity as well as the support-providing server for other units. Each unit has autonomy and specific targets. The units work in partnership where that is mutually beneficial, but compete with each other as well. Acer went so far as to split off its components, multimedia, and communications unit as a separate company, BenQ. Acer and BenQ now compete and cooperate as separate companies under the umbrella of the Acer Group.

Reconciling people centrality and result centrality. The idea is that through caring for employees' needs and introducing "treat employees kindly" as a basic value for management, individuals will feel like owners of the organization and take accountability for performance.

Reconciling rational and inspirational. Combining rational business analysis and charismatic leadership.

Reconciling hierarchical and egalitarian. The Chinese expression "rather the head of a chicken than the tail of an ox" reflects that the Chinese, although used to hierarchical structures, prefer to be their own bosses. Acer has reconciled this dimension, stimulating and rewarding entrepreneurial achievement by offering opportunities to win responsibility for a small business within the company. This has created a decentralized environment, in which the vision of top management has to receive everyone's consent.

Reconciling internal drive and responsiveness. Acer"s "go game strategy" is a perfect example of reconciliation between internal drive (building on its own strengths) and responsiveness (responding to the situation in the environment). In the traditional Chinese board game of go, the best strategy is to build a strong position in the corners and then wait for an opportunity to conquer the center. Acer adopted a globalization strategy in which it started in small, but growing, markets which were not immediately interesting for the big players and where it could win with less resources. Thus they managed to obtain top market positions in countries such as South Africa, Malaysia, the Middle East, India, Russia, and several Latin American countries.

Reconciling dynamic change and stable continuity. Speed has always been Acer's secret formula but it was reconciled with precise timing: speeding up time to market of new products and components, yet getting them there "just in time."

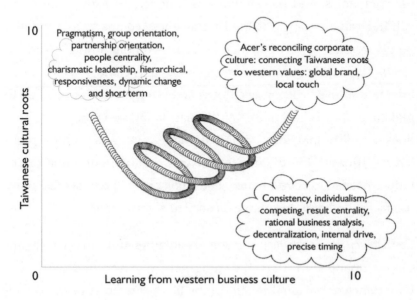

Figure 4.7 Acer's reconciling corporate culture – connecting Taiwanese cultural roots to western values

Acer has become one of the survivors in its highly competitive industry by establishing a corporate culture which is connected to its cultural roots and by combining the strengths of this traditional culture with the strengths of western values in a continuous reconciliation process (Figure 4.7).

Sony

Sony is arguably Japan's most internationalized company and one of the best known global brand names. It is often described as a kind of maverick among the big Japanese companies, as if its culture were distinctively un-Japanese (Morita, 1996). However, when we take a close look at Sony's corporate culture and how it has developed over time, we can see that it had and still has many characteristics with roots in Japanese cultural values. What makes Sony unique is that it has been more open to diversity among its people than other Japanese companies, and has shown a willingness to learn from other cultural values. Sony was the first Japanese company to appoint a non-Japanese as CEO of their American operations, in 1972 (Nathan, 1999). This has helped Sony reconcile Japanese and western value orientations in its corporate culture, and put it in a better position to globalize than other, more traditional, Japanese companies. This does not mean that Sony's international growth was without problems – after all, the dilemmas between the different value orientations needed to be reconciled. Let's look at the dilemmas that Sony has faced, and how they have reconciled some of them.

Consistency versus pragmatism. Sony is no different from other Japanese companies in that the pragmatism associated with the importance of personal relationships lies at the heart of the corporate culture. In fact, one can say that personal connections have been the source of Sony's strengths in design and innovation. The close relationship between Sony's first leaders Morita and Ibuka, who were able to communicate without words and shared much in their work and personal lives, is famous. However, Sony was the first Japanese company to realize the importance of the other side of the cultural dimension: consistency in terms of a global brand name and the image of premium quality. Although this helped to make a quick start in many business activities, the importance of personal relationships in business deals characteristic for a company like Sony caused many problems when it came to investing in the US. Even in the acquisition of Columbia Pictures, in 1989, personal relationships between the key players had a decisive role. This informality of handling big deals is not unusual in Japan but carries enormous risks in the US. In the first place, it resulted in Sony paying too much for this acquisition. In the second, it came as a complete surprise for Sony's managers that, in an American business setting, the same people who discuss a business deal in a friendly way with you one day can threaten to sue you the next. In Japan people discuss contractual problems in a personal meeting. In the third place, Sony's American executives tended to combine the advantages of American business culture (personal power and high salaries) with the advantages of Japanese corporate culture: relative autonomy and independence as long as the relationship with the boss is good. Japanese management hardly exercised any control on excessive spending by American executives in Sony's American entertainment business. In the end, these experiences have helped the company in introducing some of the strengths of American management to Sony culture, including stricter budget control and a reduced dependence on personal relationships.

Individualism versus group orientation. Sony also does not differ from other Japanese companies in that family connections in the company and expectations of loyalty played a major role in its early years.

Akio Morita's personality has had a major influence on how Sony reconciled this cultural dimension. Morita, co-author of the famous book *The Japan that Can Say No*, was known for his ability to act independently, and to be spontaneous and direct, making him the right person to handle the more individualistic, confrontational style of the US. Under his influence, Sony appointed managers in its American operations who were almost opposite to the typical Japanese manager: aggressive and very direct in expressing their individual opinions. This was not without problems because these managers showed little loyalty and sometimes ignored their Japanese bosses when they got the chance. But for Sony this was an opportunity to incorporate other strengths of American management into the Sony culture, such as reward systems that stimulate individual initiative.

Competing versus partnership. Sony was a pioneer in building alliances, such as the alliance with Philips in the 1960s, and used these partnerships to survive the cut-throat competition with its Japanese rivals such as Matsushita.

People centrality versus result centrality. People centrality was already inherent when Sony was founded, judging from the company's purpose statement formulated at the time: "Create an ideal workplace, free, dynamic, and joyous where dedicated engineers will be able to realize their craft and skills at the highest possible level." For Sony's founder Ibuka, profit was not the first motive; rather it was about establishing a workplace where engineers could enjoy technological innovation. This people orientation has been the basis of Sony's innovative strength. The American managers hired by Sony brought in different values: toughness, bottom-line focus, and reduced attention to people issues. The confrontation has been a learning experience, leading to a culture of motivating people to reach clearly defined targets.

Rational versus inspirational. Sony's "founding statement" was also about inspiring people and making them passionate. The tendency to take decisions based on emotions, typical of Sony, is not uncommon in Japan. Even in the Columbia Pictures deal, sentimental motives (such as Morita's dream of owning a movie studio) played a significant role, not just rational ones. The introduction of the Walkman, which turned out to be a great success, was a purely intuitive decision. No market testing had been done prior to launching the product. The American executives hired by Sony to manage American operations had a different way of working, one based more on rational business logic. Sony's current CEO Nobuyuki Idei reconciled this corporate culture dimension when he came up with his concept of "digital dream kids" (www.sony.net), combining an inspirational vision with rational business analysis.

Hierarchical versus egalitarian. Sony's corporate culture was originally not very different from that of most Japanese companies on this cultural dimension. Sony's first leaders Ibuka, Morita, and Ohga were all rather autocratic. In its American operations, Sony soon found out that there was less acceptance of hierarchical relationships; on the contrary, insubordination towards those in authority was not uncommon. Current CEO Nobuyuki Idei has announced that he looks for people who have unorthodox views and the courage to challenge leadership. He is looking for leaders who combine decisiveness with a willingness to listen to dissenting views.

Internal drive versus responsiveness. Sony's culture has never fitted the Japanese cultural stereotype of "being good at imitating western technology." Sony's early success was already based on a reconciliation between responsiveness (a gift for foreseeing product applications for new technologies, for attractive design, ingenuity in miniaturization) and internal drive (pioneering spirit, creating unique Sony solutions, determination to create markets and control them). Sony has always shown a willingness to take risks and to pioneer markets before there was a proven demand; for example, with the pocket-sized transistor radio, the CD, and the Walkman.

Dynamic change versus stable continuity. Sony has also never fitted the image of the Japanese company as one which was oriented towards continuous improvement in small steps. Sony's culture has always been more dynamic, based on youthful energy and a willingness to challenge the status quo. A famous story is one of how Sony started to produce transistors while the R&D project to improve manufacturing process control had not yet been finished. Idei has launched the concept of "regeneration" (www.sony.net): being revolutionary and conservative at the same time.

Long-term thinking versus short-term thinking. Sony's leadership is characterized by long-term thinking. For instance, Morita the "visionary" and Ohga the "artist" can be credited for having foreseen the convergence between hardware and software. Detailed planning has not been the strength of Sony's corporate culture. Another lesson learned from Sony's American experiences was the need for an American-style corporate planning function.

Although Sony has clearly learnt from the problems it encountered during its globalization processes, its CEO since 1995, Idei, still faces the challenge of turning the company's culture into a real reconciling corporate culture. It is not yet clear how the strengths of personal connections that have been crucial for Sony's success will be reconciled with stricter budget control and focus on results.

The cases discussed in this chapter show how corporate cultures with roots in such diverse cultures as Sweden, France, the Netherlands, Finland, the US, Taiwan, and Japan need to develop reconciling corporate cultures, based on the experiences in their globalization processes, in order to be successful in an environment with more cultural diversity. National cultural background remains important as a factor in determining corporate cultures, even of very globalized corporations. Reconciliation involves learning from local cultural values in order to improve the global corporate culture – and is a continuous process.

CHAPTER 5

Corporate culture and success…or failure

THE MYTH OF THE STRONG, HOMOGENOUS CORPORATE CULTURE AS A RECIPE FOR SUCCESS

As we discussed in the first chapter, in the debate about corporate culture as a success factor, strong cultures are often wrongly equated with homogenous or even cult-like cultures. Having one homogenous corporate culture is not just unrealistic, it is undesirable as well. Homogenous cultures can easily become complacent and incompatible with an organization's changing environment, or suffer from a lack of creativity. Moreover, many so-called strong corporate cultures are only seemingly homogenous. In reality, one subculture often dominates, for instance Marketing, R&D, Manufacturing, Finance, a particular business unit, geographical region, or a certain hierarchical level which may even be just the CEO and his or her cultural values. Lack of communication across subcultures because of imbalanced power relations leads to cultures where people are trapped into certain behaviors because they stop listening to bad news. In such a situation, other subcultures must be strengthened, unless they represent underground subcultures that look back at the comfortable, "good old" times with regret.

In our view, having a strong corporate culture means reconciling the dilemma between having a homogenous culture on the one hand and having a differentiated culture with vibrant subcultures on the other. Taking differentiation to the extreme is also undesirable. Differentiated cultures can become fragmented and indecisive because different subcultures fight with each other. In a reconciling corporate culture there is healthy rivalry between different subcultures. Reconciliation between homogenous and differentiated culture implies developing a shared commitment to aim high, which can be reflected in a set of core values shared across subcultures, business units, and regional/national culture differences. It also implies allowing and even stimulating each subculture to be a source of new, emerging values and to propose different initiatives and directions for where the company should be heading. In short, reconciling homogenous and differentiated cultures is a process of integrating diversity.

CREATIVITY AS DIVERSITY

The process of continuous learning in the interaction between global corporate culture and local/regional subcultures in the international context which we discussed in Chapter 4 is such a process of integrating diversity. However, it applies to other aspects of corporate culture as well. Take, for instance, how companies incorporate creativity into their corporate cultures. Many companies choose to keep creative departments or projects isolated from their mainstream corporate culture, because they have experienced a situation in which creative processes were easily overpowered by management control processes. Creative processes supposedly only survive in a subculture characterized by open communication, cooperation, and flexibility. However, keeping creativity separated from "mainstream" corporate culture is not a reconciliation. The challenge of integrating diversity lies in incorporating creativity into mainstream corporate culture.

General Electric

Take General Electric, the company that was – over a long period – the most frequently quoted example of a strong corporate culture, a corporate-American cultural icon. Interestingly enough former CEO

Jack Welch himself made an appeal for integrated diversity when he was transforming the company in the 1980s and 90s (Welch, 2001). Under Welch integrated diversity was the driving force behind increased interaction and cross-fertilization between business units. As Welch once said, one corporate culture does not mean one style.

The business unit GE Capital, which had been a more or less ignored segment of the company, is a case in point. GE brought in leaders from its industrial business to turn GE Capital from a purely financial business unit into a business which combined the creativity of the financial deal makers with the operational skills of the mainstream corporate culture. The leaders from the industrial business brought systems which forced a disciplined way of working, such as the Six Sigma quality system, to financial services. On the other hand, GE Capital took the lead in globalization and became the growth engine of GE because of its strengths in entrepreneurship, creativity, imagination, and a passion for deal making. GE Capital is an example of how creativity and management control processes from manufacturing and finance can be successfully reconciled.

The term integrated diversity even seems to be applicable to Welch's own career. When he became GE's CEO in 1980, after having spent most of his career outside of GE's headquarters, he had the reputation of being 180 degrees away from what was then the "model GE executive" (Slater, 1993). In the process of becoming a cultural hero at GE, he seems to have integrated his own diversity as well. So it is fair to say that GE has a strong culture, not because it's a completely homogenous culture, but because it works at an ongoing process of integrating diversity.

Philips Electronics

Now let's look at Philips Electronics, the Dutch company. When it embarked on the Centurion corporate culture change program in 1990, it was a very fragmented company. The technology-oriented side and the marketing side didn't work well together, with great innovations that often failed commercially being the result. This situation was deeply embedded in the corporate culture: of the two Philips brothers who founded the company; one (Gerard) was technology oriented and the other (Anton) more commercially oriented. Over time, the technology culture had been on the winning side. Philips definitely still had a strong corporate culture when it ran into problems at the end of the 1980s, but it had become complacent. It was satisfied with technological leadership, while forgetting financial discipline, customer orientation, and speed in bringing new products to the market.

Starting in 1990, Philips tried for more than ten years to strengthen the position of the commercial and marketing side of the company by bringing in CEOs with a commercial and marketing background, as well as by stressing customer orientation and keeping commitments as essential elements of its corporate culture. The result was not the development of a strong customer-oriented culture, but a fight between the marketing culture on the one hand and the technology culture on the other. Recently Philips has renewed its corporate values. "Delight customers" and "deliver on commitments" are still on the list. But a new one is "depend on each other," which includes "seek to understand, acknowledge, and build on others' ideas" and "help others and ask for support in delivering value" (www.philips.com). Hopefully for Philips, these values will help in developing a corporate culture which integrates the diverse strengths of its technology and marketing subcultures.

A corporate culture which is viable in the long term must address the tension and find the balance between the seemingly contradictory values of different parts of the organization, such as the technology and marketing subcultures in Philips and the finance and manufacturing subcultures at GE.

CORPORATE CULTURE AND SUCCESS

In attempts to relate corporate culture to success, the focus has been all too often on corporate cultures that help in creating short-term value for shareholders. We take a different approach to corporate culture and success. Answering the question of what kind of corporate cultures enhance long-term success in terms of economic performance, involves more than just creating short-term value for shareholders. We also need to look at success in terms of creating value for customers, success in terms of attracting and retaining top people, success in terms of building relationships with communities, and success in terms of the sustainable management of environmental resources.

The dilemma here is that on the one hand a corporate culture needs to fit the company's business strategy and business environment, so that corporate culture and value proposition are aligned, while on the other hand corporate cultures need to be adaptable to a changing environment. Unique value propositions must change to remain unique and to remain aligned with developments in the business environment as well. The challenge is to develop a corporate culture that can recognize change in the environment, and which has the versatility to implement new ways of working and new value propositions while retaining the core; we have called this "continuity through renewal."

Previous attempts to link corporate culture and success suggest either customer-oriented cultures, result-oriented cultures, people-oriented cultures or cultures of innovation as the answer. None of these acknowledge that we are dealing with dilemmas. A corporate culture that takes customer orientation (responsiveness) to the extreme may recognize changes in the market, but may also be too late in developing the proper response. If a corporate culture takes result centrality to the extreme, it will cut costs in reaction to a more difficult business environment, ultimately leading to a lack of motivation among its people to develop a new proposition to the customer. If a corporate culture takes people centrality to the extreme, it may lead to "hugging each other into bankruptcy." And if a corporate culture takes a culture of innovation (internal drive) to the extreme, it may end up spending money on developing value propositions that nobody wants.

In a reconciling culture, this works like the situation shown in Figure 5.1: because the company cares about its customers, its products, its communities, and its environment, it recognizes change in markets, in technology, and in the environment at large. Because the company

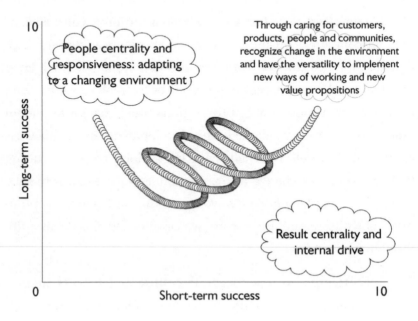

Figure 5.1 Reconciling short-term and long-term success

146

cares for both its people and its long-term survival, it continuously invests in new products/service developments and in its employees so that they are empowered and motivated to change and adapt.

Success in the airline industry: Southwest Airlines

The best example of how a corporate culture focused on results and internal drive can lead to ignoring a changing environment perhaps comes from the airline industry. The big airlines seem to have developed cultures that ignore both the needs of customers and the motivation of employees, and have not been able to react to the changing environment in which low-cost carriers are starting to play a leading role. Let's look at how the pioneer of the low-cost carriers, Southwest Airlines, reinvented air travel and developed a corporate culture that is an essential contribution to its competitive advantage. It found a market niche that the big airlines did not see, and developed a reconciling corporate culture that fitted the exploitation of this niche.

Southwest Airlines is a remarkable success in the airline industry in terms of long-term profitability, in being high on the lists of best companies to work for, and in keeping customers happy. Its corporate culture is an essential part of this success. Part of this is that the corporate culture fits the business model of low fares, no assigned seats, no on-board frills, no first class, the use of secondary airports, high utilization of aircraft, a standardized fleet, and a casual atmosphere on board. It fits the image of a company that fights for the interests of ordinary people by offering low fares. Southwest uses its marketing campaigns to promote its products, but also its culture of caring about people, and of humor and fun.

Although Southwest is not the type of company that codifies its norms and values in written documents, we can derive these from

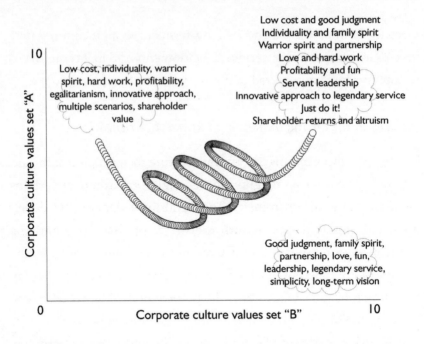

Figure 5.2 Southwest Airlines – reconciling nine corporate culture dimensions

what Southwest's long-term CEO Herb Kelleher and others have said about the culture (Freiberg and Freiberg, 1996; Kelleher, 1999; Colvin and Huey, 1999; Booker, 2001; Gittell, 2002). It turns out that Southwest fits the reconciling culture on all nine dimensions of our corporate culture model, as described below and shown in Figure 5.2.

Consistency versus pragmatism. Southwest values combine low cost and common sense/good judgement. Consistency in service concept and offering low fares is reconciled with encouraging frontline staff to use their own judgement and common sense above simple adherence to rules.

Individuality versus group orientation. Southwest values combine individuality and family spirit. Encouraging staff to think and act like mavericks is reconciled with family spirit.

Competing versus partnership. Southwest keeps up a "warrior spirit" and is aggressive in the battle with competition, including in its advertising campaigns, but combines this with strong partnerships with suppliers, customers, and authorities because it consistently proves that it keeps its promises.

People centrality versus result centrality. Southwest values combine love and hard work. Through treating employees with care, showing concern for them, pride in them, and trusting them (a forgive and forget culture), it also motivates them to deliver results.

Rational versus inspirational. Here Southwest values combine profitability and fun. Through inspiring people by celebrations of success and creating an image of creativity, play, and humor it reaches the rational goal of profitability.

Egalitarianism versus hierarchical. One of the Southwest values is egalitarianism: Leadership is not a position of power and authority or title at Southwest. The personal philosophy of former CEO Herb Kelleher about leadership is probably the ultimate reconciliation on this dimension: servant leadership, or leadership through collaborative relationships.

Internal drive versus responsiveness. Responsiveness is the key to what Southwest calls its "legendary service" – treating customers with respect and kindness. However, the image of legendary service has been created through a determined, innovative approach to make Southwest uniquely different from other airlines.

Stable continuity versus dynamic change. Southwest values include simplicity and keeping multiple scenarios, thereby reconciling planning for a variety of possible developments and implementing changes in a speedy and informal way. Southwest's "Just do it!" culture dates back to the very start of the company when it found a market niche and jumped into it.

Short term versus long term. Southwest combines attention for shareholder returns with ownership (sharing the financial benefits of ownership with employees), altruism (dedication to long lasting relationships with communities, etc.), and the long-term vision of making it possible to fly at low fares.

Continuously reconciling its corporate culture seems to be a crucial factor in the success of Southwest Airlines, and was part of the reason why its recent leadership change did not cause too much turmoil.

Starbucks

Another company with a corporate culture that has contributed to its amazing success story in terms of profitability, commitment of its people, and reputation as a fair business is the Starbucks Coffee Company. It started in 1971 with a small store in Seattle selling coffee beans and now has more than 7,000 retail outlets in North America, Latin America, Europe, the Middle East, and the Pacific Rim. Integrating cultural diversity is definitely at the heart of Starbucks' success: it integrated the Italian coffee bar culture with American marketing and service concepts to give a global success formula. But Starbucks corporate culture is at the heart of its success as well, if only in how it manages to avoid being seen as just another example of "American fast food domination."

Starbucks CEO Howard Schultz has paid a lot of attention to shaping Starbucks' corporate culture because he realizes that employees will be only motivated to make a company a success if the company they work for is meaningful to them (Schultz, 1997; 1999). When we

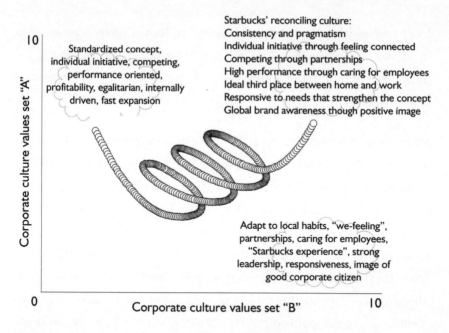

10

Corporate culture values set "A"

Standardized concept, individual initiative, competing, performance oriented, profitability, egalitarian, internally driven, fast expansion

Starbucks' reconciling culture:
Consistency and pragmatism
Individual initiative through feeling connected
Competing through partnerships
High performance through caring for employees
Ideal third place between home and work
Responsive to needs that strengthen the concept
Global brand awareness though positive image

Adapt to local habits, "we-feeling", partnerships, caring for employees, "Starbucks experience", strong leadership, responsiveness, image of good corporate citizen

0

Corporate culture values set "B"

10

Figure 5.3   Starbucks – reconciling nine corporate culture dimensions

look at Starbucks corporate culture, it becomes clear that it fits the reconciling corporate culture concept as shown in Figure 5.3. Let's look at this in more detail.

Consistency versus pragmatism. Part of Starbucks' culture is the standardized concept, the global brand, the premium quality (and premium price) and the measures to keep up standards of quality and service, for instance by training sessions for newly hired employees and global training for local branch managers. In every outlet you can expect the same high-quality coffee, made from the best beans. However, although the standardized concept resembles a fast food culture with its self-service concept, Starbucks manages to keep a personalized touch to the atmosphere. Starbucks' best practice rule implies that all their outlets are encouraged to come up with new ideas and to share them with other outlets worldwide. Starbucks allows its local operations to adapt in a pragmatic way to local coffee-drinking habits and tastes, to local preferences for the locations of their outlets, to some extent to local price levels and to local ways of motivating employees. Thus, consistency and pragmatism are reconciled.

Reconciliation, however, is a continuous process. Although Starbucks was initially very successful in Asia, part of this success was due to not to its coffee but to curiosity about a new, foreign environment. Now that local competitors have learned the concept, they can start challenging Starbucks by lower pricing, offering a more attractive outlook and better food quality, or by offering a more traditional form of Asian hospitality and a less overcrowded atmosphere. Recently Starbucks moved into France, seemingly the most challenging culture for standardized approaches because of the French demand for uniqueness. However, this offers new opportunities for reconciliation as well; France has a long standing tradition in which cafés are historically associated with meeting places for authors, philosophers, and artists.

Individualism versus group orientation. Having a cohesive group behind the counter at each store is of the essence in Starbucks' service concept, but individual initiative is stimulated too. Many initiatives for new products and services have come from individual employees. Selling an iced coffee beverage, now called the Frappuccino, was an initiative from an employee who had requests from customers for cold drinks on a hot summer day; selling specially compiled CDs, containing the music played in the outlets, is based on the idea of an employee who was asked by customers where they could buy the music that was playing in the store. Starbucks' mission statement – "Provide a great work environment where we treat each other with respect and dignity" – reflects the reconciliation between individualism and group orientation:

employees are treated in a way that makes them feel connected with the company. Managers refer to employees, both full-time and part-time, as partners, and in a way they are treated like partners. Since 1990 Starbucks has a stock option plan for all its partners.

Competing versus partnership. Starbucks started its expansion in Europe with a major acquisition in the UK. It changed to a partner-ship-oriented strategy after its first experiences in expanding to continental Europe, where discussions with the management of a Swiss company showed that the Swiss managers were hesitant because they expected Starbucks' competitive approach to be too aggressive for Swiss culture. Finally they chose a form of cooper-ation more in line with the idea of integrating diversity. Starbucks formed a joint venture with its Swiss partner in which Swiss manag-ers maintained control of front-line operations, such as dealing with customers and employees, and the American management focused on linking the local operations to the global network.

Starbucks has used this partnership model in its further globaliza-tion process. For instance, Starbucks entered Spain by working with a Spanish partner and began its operations in France as a joint ven-ture with this Spanish partner. Starbucks has developed many other partnerships, including partnerships to get access to non-traditional retail sites (with airlines, cruise lines, and bookstores), partnerships to comarket products (with Dreyers in ice-cream and with PepsiCo for the Frappuccino product) and partnerships to offer innovative services (e.g., an alliance with HP and T-mobile to offer wireless internet services in Starbucks outlets). Thus Starbucks reconciles its competitive, aggressive expansion strategy with building partner-ships all over the globe.

People centrality versus result centrality. The main reason for the hesi-tance of Starbucks' acquisition target in Switzerland was that they saw Starbucks as driven by results, leading to increasing demands for quicker service, maximum output, more stress, and greater personal struggle for achievement. Local management was afraid that employees would be fired if their performance was not in line with the Starbucks model, or that they would become demotivated which would lead to customer complaints. It took some time before they appreciated that caring for employees and treating them as partners was part of Starbucks' culture. Thus through caring for employees, Starbucks reaches high levels of productivity and performance.

Rational versus inspirational. Starbucks tries to provide more to the customer than just coffee. The corporate culture is designed to offer a total "Starbucks Experience" (www.starbucks.com). You can buy compact discs and coffee-making equipment and additional "experience" is continuously added, for instance by offering access to wireless broadband internet service in the outlets. The rational goal of profitability is reached through being inspirational. In fact, as is well known, Starbucks tries to position itself as the ideal third place between home and work, the ultimate reconciliation of this dimension.

Egalitarian versus hierarchical. Starbucks has a very flat organizational structure. Most employees start at the lowest level in a relatively low-skilled job, but anyone at Starbucks can reach a higher position if they work hard. Even so Starbucks has a hierarchical side as well, with long term CEO Shultz as the father figure in the Starbucks family. The reconciliation in Starbucks corporate culture is to keep the same level of trust and confidence in management decisions as if it were still a small company.

Internal drive versus responsiveness. Starbucks can be extremely internally driven when implementing its concept. When the company started in Japan, it was advised to keep the outlets small because of high rents, to create smoking areas in the outlets, and not to offer "coffee-to-go" because drinking on the street would supposedly mean a loss of face for the Japanese. Starbucks followed none of this advice because it did not fit its service concept. Still, it did show responsiveness by following the advice of its local partner to make adaptations to the Japanese environment that did not conflict with the service concept, for instance offering unique products – such as the Green Tea Frappuccino – and non-coffee merchandising. Starbucks was initially very successful with this reconciliation of internal drive and responsiveness in Japan, but again has to realize that reconciliation is a continuous process. Local competitors have already copied the concept while making increased adaptations to the Japanese environment, for instance by allowing their customers to smoke. When Starbucks started in China it took a similar approach. There was no coffee-drinking habit in China, so Starbucks created their own "coffee culture." However, they did make a link to the sense of community and the "surrogate living room" atmosphere of the existing tea house culture, and translated it to bringing people together through coffee. Offering board games for customers to play may look like an innovation in the US, but it's a Chinese tea house tradition.

Stable continuity versus dynamic growth and *short-term versus long-term orientation*. Starbucks has expanded fast and in a profitable way, but its corporate culture is more long-term oriented than most American corporate cultures. Starbucks' management promotes what they call "endurance" in order to convince its shareholders to think of more than just short-term profitability. One of the things that Starbucks have done to ensure long-term growth and profitability is to build stable relationships with its coffee bean producers right from the start. It pays a margin of up to 50 percent on coffee prices to its Latin American growers and assists in the sustainable growth of their local economy by environmental programs and building communities. Paying "fair trade" prices, of course, helps Starbucks to improve its image as a good corporate and global citizen, which in turn adds to global brand awareness.

CORPORATE SOCIAL RESPONSIBILITY AND SUCCESS

Corporate social responsibility means more than adding "caring for the environment," "being a good corporate citizen," or "supporting sustainable development" to a list of corporate values. Corporate social responsibility should be more than reputation management to keep environmental groups and non governmental organizations at bay. Incorporating corporate social responsibility into a corporate culture requires solving the dilemma of short-term orientation and long-term caring for all stakeholders by taking the social and environmental impact of doing business into account. Just as listening to staff and customers have become more and more important elements of corporate culture (reflected in the "people centrality" and "responsiveness" orientations in the corporate culture dimensions), listening to all stakeholders including surrounding communities is also rapidly becoming an important element of corporate culture, with a big impact on competitive advantage and success. Taking a proactive stand in social and environmental issues by starting a dialogue with all stakeholders is actually a first step in a reconciliation process that leads to creating win–win solutions.

Not all companies recognize that there is a dilemma here. However, it is realistic to say that taking the social and environmental impact of business into account can become a negative when a company limits itself to an isolated initiative. (Ignoring social and environmental impact can then become a short-term competitive advantage for a competitor who is willing to take on the "dirty" business.) The other extreme, short-term shareholder orientation (not taking the social/environmental impact into account – or being perceived as not taking it into account) can become a negative as well.

Oil companies and corporate social responsibility

Oil companies are the obvious example of companies which have to deal with this dilemma, because of the environmental effect of pipelines, etc., and the social effect of displaced populations in areas where they are active. Shell experienced this when, in 1995, it wanted to sink the Brent Spar oil storage rig in the North Sea, leading to a massive protest from environmental groups and the public at large (Spyckerelle and Hampden-Turner, 2001). Shell was also blamed by human rights activists in 1995 for not intervening in host-country politics when Ken Saro-Wiwa was executed in Nigeria. Saro-Wiwa was a human rights activist and the representative of the Nigerian tribe which felt that Shell had been negligent in its environmental and humanitarian responsibilities in the region where it had been drilling for 30 years.

The general dilemma of corporate responsibility is plotted in Figure 5.4. Reconciliation of this dilemma involves dialogue with communities, activists, and NGOs to gather input from all external stakeholders in order to take a proactive stand on issues of social/ environmental impact, setting the stage in environmental and human rights principles and turning this to competitive advantage. This requires a corporate culture that is willing to listen to the outside world and is able to respond to views of stakeholders. Successful reconciliation of the dilemma of how to balance environmental/ social issues with business needs requires reconciliation on other corporate culture dimensions as well:

• Reconciliation of the rational versus inspirational dimension:

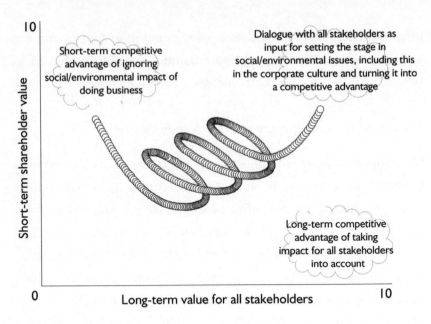

Figure 5.4 Corporate social responsibility dilemma

internal communication to create a corporate culture that values purpose not just in terms of business results, but also in societal terms.

- Reconciliation of the people centrality versus result centrality dimension: establishment of performance measures that connect performance in monetary terms and also in terms of social development.

- Reconciling the internal drive versus responsiveness dimension: openness for evaluating company strategy in terms of business outcomes and broader social impact with external stakeholders.

- Reconciling the competing versus partnership orientation dimension: building trust with critical external stakeholders to enter a dialogue and to build strategic partnerships while remaining independent of each other.

- Reconciling the egalitarian versus hierarchical dimension:

openness to linking external stakeholder involvement to strategic decision making by installing advisory councils in which different stakeholders participate and which have decision-making power.

Oil companies are indeed at the forefront of developing corporate cultures of corporate responsibility that help them to achieve competitive advantage and success. BP uses the slogan "Beyond Petroleum" as a symbol for its effort to combine building a business with sensitivity to environmental issues, for instance by being a leader in solar energy technology. BP and Shell both take a proactive stand in the debate about climate change and impose targets on themselves based on the Kyoto agreement to reduce greenhouse gas emissions. Shell has formulated a number of business principles to embed corporate social responsibility in its corporate culture and is one of the companies that introduced "triple bottom line" reporting: it produces financial, environmental, and social year reports. These address the performance indicators related to acceptability of environmental performance and human rights, and to the perception of the stakeholders about the quality of Shell's engagement.

Banks and corporate responsibility

The oil industry is by no means the only one that needs to deal with including corporate responsibility in its corporate culture. Take international banks. NGOs accuse banks of financing companies that do business in an irresponsible way; for example, mining companies that extract minerals, destroy forests, and exploit workers. The banks are increasingly seen as accomplices of these companies and therefore become targets of protests themselves. Ignoring protest by stating "what our customers do is not our business" is no solution. Backing out as soon as corporate reputation is at stake is

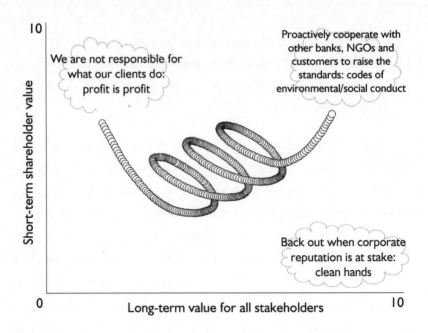

Figure 5.5 Corporate social responsibility dilemma for international banks

also not a satisfactory solution: this would be interpreted as not caring for the customer. The dilemma is depicted in Figure 5.5. Reconciliation involves a dialogue with customers, NGOs, and other financial institutions in order to codevelop environmental/social codes of conduct. Through codeveloping improved environmental/social standards, banks can raise the standards of what is acceptable, thereby taking responsibility for who their customers are – and, in the end, gaining competitive advantage over other financial bodies that do not comply with the new standards.

For example, in June 2003, ten international project finance banks, including ABN Amro, Dresdner Bank, and Barclays, adopted the Equator Principles. These are based on World Bank group environmental and social guidelines, policies,and procedures, raising the standards for project finance and achieving a level playing field among project financing banks in the field of environmental and social risk management (www. equator-principles.com). The Equator Principles imply that the participating banks commit themselves to not providing funds for controversial projects.

The examples in this section show that reconciling corporate cultures on all cultural dimensions have a high propensity for success, not just in terms of profitability, but also in creating value for customers, being seen as attractive employers, and in terms of contributing to a sustainable society.

CORPORATE CULTURE AND FAILURE

Strong corporate cultures are not a guaranteed recipe for success. As we discussed in Chapter 1, corporate culture is maybe even more associated with failure than with success nowadays. Reconciling corporate values is by no means easy. A corporate culture might get stuck at one extreme because a subculture becomes dominant due to (temporary) success. The reconciliation spiral might even go downward (to the "0,0" position) because of conflict or lack of adaptation to changing environments. What are the mechanisms that can make corporate cultures turn into low-performance cultures, or even lead to corporate cultures characterized by fear, denial, cynicism, self-interest, or distrust? And what guidelines can be given in order to avoid the origination of a low-performance culture?

Arthur Andersen, Enron, WorldCom, and Ahold are some of the notable recent examples of companies that (almost) went down because their corporate culture allowed or even encouraged behaviors that were either illegal, not in line with codes of conduct, or that led to taking unacceptable risks or pursuing self-interest. Even whole industries can be hit by the unhealthy culture virus. In 2002 a parliamentary investigation in the Netherlands on practices in the construction industry revealed that illegal price agreements between competitors, cartel forming, and informal meetings in which markets were divided were all deeply ingrained in the culture of the Dutch building industry. Governments and municipal authorities (an important customer of the building industry) and the general public felt cheated, which led to a bad business climate for the building industry in general.

It is not fair to blame every individual who works for a company with an unhealthy culture. Even in companies that went down because some of their people showed behaviors not in line with integrity, the large majority of employees were honest people. However, it cannot be denied that corporate cultures can develop in which people – out of fear for the consequences, out of self-interest or downright cynicism – ignore dubious practices or bending the rules. Just adding "integrity" to your list of core values and claiming that you have a strong culture of integrity won't help. In all companies people face dilemmas, and the corporate culture needs to help them resolve these in order to prevent an unhealthy culture from developing.

Let's look in more detail at the corporate cultures of two companies that undoubtedly developed unhealthy cultures: Arthur Andersen and Enron.

Arthur Andersen

Arthur Andersen used to appear on lists of companies with a strong culture. This strong corporate culture can be traced back to its start as an audit company. It upheld its culture by hiring young people, training them in the "Andersen way" of conducting business and in the standards for conducting audit processes, and by imposing behavioral standards such as dress codes. It managed to keep a "one firm" culture when it globalized (Squires et al, 2003; Toffler and

Reingold, 2003). This corporate culture was very much a "consistency" culture: its value of professionalism implied using standard methods, standard quality norms, and standard ways of doing business, which included integrity and honesty. This was reinforced by the clear hierarchy of its partnership structure.

Arthur Andersen's old culture could be assessed on our nine dimensions of corporate culture as characterized by consistency, group orientation (loyalty and conformity to the firm), competing, result centrality, a rational "work hard/play hard" culture, respect for hierarchical ranks, internally driven as in "think straight/talk straight", and as long-term, stable, continuity orientated, aimed at serving the public good. Seemingly no dilemmas here – this strong culture was actually considered to be a unique asset, although some would describe this type of corporate culture as tending to be over-confident and arrogant.

Things started to change when the dominance of the audit practice was challenged by another subculture, Andersen's consulting practice, which became very successful in the 1990s. Probably the most important cultural difference was that while for the accountants, the corporate value of customer orientation still included the internally driven attitude of "do everything to make sure that the client complies with all regulatory requirements," for the consultants, customer orientation started to mean "do everything to satisfy the customer so that we continue to get high fees and can meet our stretched results targets." Now there was a dilemma because the interpretation of the consultants' culture seemed to lead to a conflict with the "consistency" culture of professionalism and integrity – systematically testing the boundaries of and loopholes in laws and regulations seemed to become acceptable. We can see no sign that the leadership of Arthur Andersen ever explicitly addressed this dilemma and tried to reconcile it. By this time the corporate culture consisted of two subcultures fighting with each other, which continued even after the consulting business was split off in 2000. The dilemma between the homogenous culture in which Arthur Andersen's culture originated and the differentiated culture that it had become was not resolved in line with our concept of integrating diversity. Instead, it became a fragmented culture, in which loyalty and conformity to the direct partner in charge kept the organization together – at least for some time.

In such a fragmented corporate culture, there is little control over who takes the value orientation of pragmatism too far and ends up in violating the norms of integrity – even if the majority of the company still follows the norm. The way in which Arthur Andersen dealt with its Enron account led to the downfall of the company. There are some reports that Andersen's Professional Standards Group did struggle with the managers responsible for the Enron account because they were unhappy with how transactions were handled. This means that an attempt to reconcile the dilemmas would still have been possible at that time. However, it seems that a culture had developed in which following the letter of the law while breaching its intentions was accepted, and helping clients to show inflated profits to the financial world was encouraged. Arthur Andersen is a perfect example of how showing a lack of leadership in stopping the development of corporate culture in the wrong direction can be fatal.

Enron

The events leading to the collapse of Enron have been often described (Fox, 2003; McLean and Elkind, 2003; Watkins and Swartz, 2003), but not from a perspective of the development of its corporate culture. Enron was heralded in the 1990s as a company in a conservative utility business which had built a modern, result-oriented corporate culture. Deregulation and privatization of the energy business, the new market for trading electricity, and Enron's enormous expansion in the mid 90s had a huge impact on its corporate culture. We can evaluate the development of Enron's corporate culture using our nine cultural dimensions as illustrated in Figure 5.6, and described below.

- Enron went from a regulated utility, valuing consistency, to a corporate culture valuing pragmatism. Entrepreneurship in the new free markets of power generation and distribution required flexibility and adaptability. A freewheeling culture developed, and as long as you made money, management didn't bother: controls were not always followed. Over time, the rules were bent more and more and in the end they were

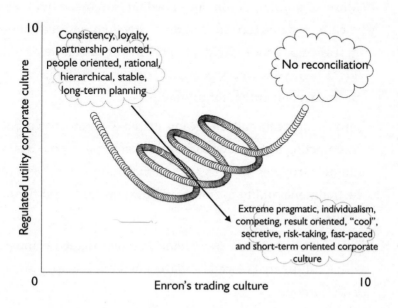

Figure 5.6 Enron corporate culture – a downward spiral instead of reconciliation

broken, encouraged by other characteristics of the corporate culture: individualism, competitiveness, result centrality, internal drive, and short-term orientation. Exemplary for this extreme "pragmatic" corporate culture are the "special purpose entity" transactions, designed in such a complex way that they could serve to keep debts off Enron's books. This corporate culture first tolerated risky accounting practices, then questionable accounting practices, and finally improper deals that led to conflicts of interest between the company and individual executives, and that violated codes of conduct. Pragmatism taken to the extreme showed up in other practices as well, such as providing inaccurate information to rating agencies and unfairly manipulating power prices by making use of poorly designed regulation plans.

- In contrast with the traditionally more collective corporate culture of utilities, Enron developed an extreme individualistic culture characterized by lots of freedom and autonomy, aggressive pay for individual performance, a culture of individual high performers going after their own interests, and cut-throat competition for promotion.

- Enron's corporate culture became extremely competitive, both in competing in the new trading market in power but also in internal struggles such as the internal competition between the traditional utility business, and the new trade and finance business.

- Enron developed into an extremely result-oriented company with a culture that placed profit first and put intense pressure on performing.

- Enron moved from the rational, analytical utility culture to a company that wanted to be seen as the world's coolest company, the ultimate example of transformation from old economy to the inspirational internet economy.

- Although Enron changed over time from a steep, hierarchical organization to a flat structure with only four hierarchical layers, this doesn't mean that it became more egalitarian. The power distance and the information gap between the hierarchical layers actually increased, leaving little view on what happened at the top level.

- Enron was very internally driven in taking the lead in making use of deregulation in its industry. It became one of the first electricity traders. In fact, it soon started to trade almost everything – including weather derivatives and bandwidth on fibre-optics networks. This pioneering culture developed into a culture of extreme self-confidence (or even arrogance) and risk taking.

- In contrast with the traditional stable, long-term, strategic-planning-oriented utility culture, Enron developed an innovative, fast-paced, dynamic and short-term oriented culture. It operated in a very volatile market, with big but risky opportunities for making profit in the trading business; it reorganized all the time to align with rapidly shifting markets, and developed a culture focused on quarterly results because of the importance of its share price for bonuses. In taking the short-term culture to the extreme, booking profits from long-term deals right away became an accepted practice.

Very swift changes in a corporate culture, as at Enron, should be a reason to be suspicious, because it indicates that one subculture is beginnning to dominate. If there still were elements of a "utility subculture" left at Enron, then it clearly was powerless. Anyway the corporate culture that developed at Enron left little room for dissent and dialogue because the top of the organization had developed an attitude of being almighty and invulnerable. Corporate cultures that combine extreme value orientations are at risk anyway, but the combination of pragmatism and individualism, as with Enron, can easily lead to a culture of greed. Enron's core values of "respect, integrity, communication, and excellence" were clearly not meaningful for the corporate culture that had developed in reality, which could be better characterized by arrogance, ruthlessness, taking no time for communication, and untrustworthiness.

The examples in this section show that developing a corporate culture which combines extreme value orientations instead of reconciling them can easily lead to failure. Developing meaningful corporate values is a process of constructive confrontation, which did not take place in a crucial phase of the developments at Arthur Andersen and Enron, caused by a lack of leadership and a lack of control of leadership respectively.

CHAPTER 6

Creating and changing a corporate culture

Two famous questions that management guru Peter Drucker recommended managers to ask themselves were "What kind of business are we?" and "What kind of business should we be?" When we talk about corporate culture change, we encourage managers to ask themselves "What kind of company are we?" and "What kind of company should we be?"

DILEMMAS IN CORPORATE CULTURE CHANGE

As discussed in Chapter 2, the process of achieving and sustaining corporate culture change has been underestimated. Change is not a matter of discarding the old culture and implementing a completely new one. Changing organizational cultures is a dilemma in itself. On the one hand, organizational cultures provide consistency, order, a core of the company that is strong and enduring.

On the other hand they need to be adaptable to a changing environment. Changing corporate cultures is about finding a balance between radical change and organic modifications, between bold moves and incremental adjustment. The dilemma of change versus stability needs to be reconciled by "dynamic stability" or "continuity through renewal." However, the pressure on companies for a rapid pace of change is enormous nowadays. Pressure from financial markets and shareholders, pressure from competition, pressure related to technological change, changing customer demands, deregulation, and emerging new business models may all require speedy change. Still, it is important to ensure that the strengths of the current corporate culture do not get lost in the process.

It is therefore necessary to know your existing culture and what you want to retain from it before embarking on a change project. For instance, if a company wanted to change from a people-centrality culture, based on good personal relationships and mutual respect between bosses and subordinates, to a more result-oriented culture, the challenge would be one of how to make use of respect for authority in order to get the work done. Or if a company wanted to change from a responsiveness culture, characterized by close relationships with the customer, to a more internally driven culture with a stronger emphasis on business processes, the challenge would be how to make use of the relationship with the client to improve the business processes.

Companies also face this dilemma of radical change versus stability when a change of leadership is required and a choice has to be made between appointing an internally developed CEO or a new CEO from outside, which will be discussed later in this chapter.

Dilemmas in the change process

Radical change versus stability is not the only dilemma in corporate culture change. Here are some other dilemmas which are inherent in the change process:

- Consensus versus decisiveness. Should everybody be allowed to participate in discussions about the change programme (as would be expected in most Scandinavian, Dutch, and German corporate cultures) or should corporate culture change be driven by top management, for instance by defining a set of core values and cascading these down? This is a dilemma that needs to be resolved. Going for one extreme, for example deciding on a set of corporate values such as "team oriented, customer oriented, performance oriented, respect for individuals, open for change, innovative, fun, entrepreneurial, and trust" does not work.
- Changing rules for behavior versus fundamental change. Can a corporate culture be changed by drafting rules or codes of

conduct, or does corporate culture change require a more fundamental approach, starting with the deeper assumptions? For instance, when a Wall Street broking firm wanted its brokers to use "cleaner language" in order to comply with regulators it issued a new code of conduct and announced that it would retain and record emails and phone calls. It is questionable whether changing the rules leads to more ethical behavior, because integrity is about deeper assumptions and not a matter of rules. Another example is that Management by Objectives (a rule-oriented instrument for change) worked in the US, but failed in France: it did not fit in with corporate cultures where letting people set their own objectives was interpreted as a sign of weakness and surrendering power.

- Change focused on cost reduction versus change focused on investments in growth and motivation. Deteriorating financial results are often the immediate trigger for change and cost cutting programs the first measures that managers consider. However, driving cost cutting programs is often not seen as very motivating by the most talented employees, who are looking for opportunities for professional and personal growth nowadays. Improving financial results also requires having a corporate culture that is attractive for these kinds of people. Therefore the dilemma of change focused on cost reduction versus on investments in growth and motivation needs to be resolved.

In our experience, corporate culture change programmes driven by imposing sets of values top-down, by drafting codes of conduct and behavioral rules without addressing the fundamental issues at the heart of undesirable behaviors, and by cost reduction programmes without investing in people, are all doomed to failure. As we discussed in the first chapter, developing meaningful corporate cultures is a process of constructive confrontation in a dialogue between all stakeholders. Later in this chapter we will introduce an approach to corporate culture change which addresses the dilemmas mentioned above by reconciling them:

- How can we ensure continuity through renewal?

- How can we, through involving people in the change program, win their commitment so that decisions will be implemented without delay?

- How can we, through paying attention to the problems and dilemmas that people face in their day-to-day work, discover the needs for fundamental change and respond appropriately in terms of bringing about changes in organization, systems, processes?

- How can we achieve cost reduction through investing in people development, e.g., training?

CREATING A CORPORATE CULTURE IN START-UP COMPANIES

The creation of corporate cultures in start-up companies, for example in the ICT industry, is often dependent on a single founder. Many companies, even when they have grown into maturity, are still built around the image of one entrepreneurial leader: think of Bill Gates at Microsoft, Richard Branson at Virgin, Jeff Bezos at Amazon, Michael Dell at Dell, Steve Jobs at Apple, John Chambers at Cisco, and Larry Ellison at Oracle. The risk of any start-up company is that the entrepreneurial culture becomes dysfunctional when the company grows into maturity – even more so when the company is dependent on one leader. The typical values of entrepreneurs – pragmatism, individualism, competing, result centrality, inspirational, internally driven, dynamic, and change oriented – can become a hindrance when they show up at a later stage in a lack of willingness to listen, resulting in the not invented here (NIH) syndrome, or in overconfidence. Some entrepreneurial leaders have two sides to them: Bill Gates turned out to be not just a computer whizz, but also a shrewd businessman and negotiator. Other companies integrate diversity by finding a balance between two leaders in an early stage of development: the creative innovator and entrepreneur with the analytical businessman, such as Michael Dell and Kevin Rollins at Dell.

Let's look in more detail at the development of the corporate culture of some start-up companies of the 1980s and 90s: Amazon.com, Boo.com, and Dell.

Amazon.com

Amazon.com is one of the few enduring success stories of the dot-com hype in the 1990s, although it still took the company seven years to begin making profit after its founding in 1994. Part of Amazon's success is that it took advantage of the fact that the importance of the corporate culture concept was already established when it was founded. Amazon founder Jeff Bezos already knew, when he started the company, that corporate culture would be a powerful force in making it happen, although he also realized that a leader can shape only a part of it. "Competitors can never copy a culture," was one of Bezos' early catchphrases (Saunders, 2001), although he had Microsoft in mind as a role model himself (Spector, 2000). So while Bezos' role as an entrepreneur was crucial, as in any start-up – the ground-breaking idea, the drive to make a difference and work extremely hard for it, the inspirational skill to attract investors, suppliers, and a first batch of dedicated co-workers – the fact that he also preached and practiced values in line with a stable and consis-

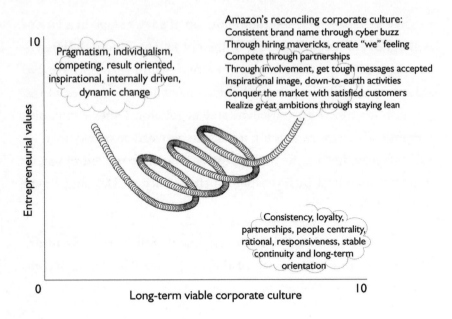

Figure 6.1 Amazon.com's corporate culture reconciliation

tent corporate culture made the difference. And when we look at Amazon's corporate culture using the nine dimensions of corporate culture, it seems that he intuitively went for the reconciling model. This is how we analyze Amazon's corporate culture on the nine dimensions (illustrated in Figure 6.1).

Consistency versus pragmatism. As one would expect from a start-up company, Amazon's corporate culture began with pragmatism. Developing customized software was necessary because there was then no standard software available for handling purchases via email or for secure credit card orders. However as soon as standard application software was available Amazon did not hesitate to make the switch. Amazon did not have the money available for marketing efforts to establish its brand name as a global standard, but created brand name recognition in a pragmatic way instead: by building a participative website that, because it was experienced as entertaining and cool, generated a community feeling among its users – the brand was established through its own customers who passed on the message to friends, colleagues, and others via the internet. Through cyber buzz thanks to exceeding customer expectations, Amazon built its brand with a relatively low investment in marketing costs.

Individualism versus group orientation. Bezos was very much aware of the fact that hiring the right people was crucial to establishing the corporate culture he wanted, so he made sure that creative individuals were recruited, people who would add to the team. Employees were given autonomy in their jobs, but Bezos put a lot of effort into promoting a sense of community. So, through hiring mavericks, a "we are Amazon" feeling, loyalty, and commitment were created.

Competing versus partnerships. Amazon started building affiliations with other websites at an early stage through its "associate program," and used this scheme as a strength in the fierce competition with Barnes & Noble that took off as soon as the traditional bookseller started to see the danger Amazon represented. Amazon competed through having the right partnerships.

People centrality versus result centrality and *egalitarian versus hierarchical.* The atmosphere at Amazon in the early years was described as intense and friendly – a combination of demanding high work ethics and offering employees dignity, respect, recognition, appreciation, involvement, and a fun working environment. Bezos managed to become known as Mr. Nice Guy while maintaining a performance-driven culture as illustrated by the catchphrase "It's Day One, we can't stop or rest" (Bernstein and Hof, 2000). However reconciliation is a continuous process. Bezos lost his Mr Nice Guy image in 2000 when he had to reduce staff numbers because investors demanded a return on their investments. As a result, employees started to complain and job security became an issue. Amazon had 8,000 employees and many did not accept the kind of working life there – still that of a recent start-up company, including long working hours, mandatory overtime, and below-market-level salaries. Amazon managed to reconcile this because, despite Bezos' strong leadership, the company had remained a democratic culture, characterized by open communication and employee participation in decision making. Through maintaining a participative and open communication culture, Amazon managed to get tough messages accepted by staff.

Rational versus inspirational. Amazon combined a focus on down-to-earth activities and a culture of frugality with the image of Bezos' inspirational brilliance.

Internal drive versus responsiveness. Amazon's early claim that it was the world's biggest bookshop could have been seen as arrogant – but at the same time the company proved its "customer-centric" culture by being responsive to non-standard customer requests and the needs of customers by analyzing their behavior on its website. Through the drive to provide superior customer services, Amazon pushed its brand and business model and conquered the market.

Stable continuity versus dynamic change and *short-term versus long-term orientation.* Although Bezos had a long-term vision for Amazon as becoming the leading internet retailer, the company took a step-by-step approach, with the goal of being the biggest bookstore on the net, thereby taking an edge in technology, logistics, and brand name. However, Amazon was not afraid to reinvent itself as fast as market changes demanded, for example when web-based customer service activity was partly shifted to India. Amazon did not fall into the trap that other dot-com start-ups fell into: short-term spending. It stayed relatively lean; Bezos still keeps a relatively small and simple office in Amazon's unassuming headquarters, for example. This has helped in keeping the investors' confidence for a number of years before the company started to make profit.

Amazon.com is still in business and even profitable after ten years and it seems that its reconciling corporate culture did make a difference. This is a big contrast with the many internet retailers that went down in the dot-com crash. Boo.com was one of the first casualties.

Boo.com

Boo.com collapsed in May 2000 after only 18 months of operation when investors stopped funding after at least $100 million of their money had been spent. The Swedish founders Ernst Malmsten and Kajsa Leander had a lot in common with Bezos. They were also young entrepreneurs, driven to make their mark with an innovative idea, in their case one of creating a world-leading, internet-based retailer of high-end sportswear and high-fashion clothes. Malmsten and Leander were also charismatic and inspirational in attracting investors, suppliers, and employees. Boo.com was a trendy start-up company with a stock market value of $400 million at the start of 2000. A few months later the business was closed and sold for about $130,000. All that is left of the brand today is a basic portal site, fashionmall.com.

Why did Boo.com not survive the dot-com shakeout around the end of the century? We argue that the company never made a serious attempt to establish a reconciling corporate culture. Its leaders were too busy being celebrity entrepreneurs and simply did not spend enough time and attention to steering the company's corporate culture. The culture that developed there was extreme on all corporate culture dimensions.

Consistency versus pragmatism. Boo.com's corporate culture was characterized by extreme pragmatism. Its management spent enormous amounts of money on public relations and on international travel with the aim of building relationships with prestigious investors, such as the Benetton family, and with the media. Boo.com was also too pragmatic in its expansion in Europe. It tried to tackle the European market by targeting 18 countries simultaneously while still being sensitive to the complexities: the different legal, tax, and regulatory systems; different currencies; different local languages; different consumer preferences; different local payment methods. For instance in Germany and Scandinavia, where people were less familiar with paying by credit card on the internet, Boo.com sent invoices instead of asking for payment upfront, leading to high extra costs. E-commerce calls for localization throughout the entire buying process, requiring an advanced technology platform in order to ensure the consistency and spreading of the brand. However, Boo.com did not invest enough in developing its technology platform, with the result that its website went live too late and was cumbersome and slow when it was finally fully live at the end of 1999. The emphasis on pragmatism ensured that Boo.com forgot to consolidate a global business structure, including the financial controls.

Individualism versus group orientation. Boo.com was characterized by extreme individualism. High-profile individuals (purchasers, art directors) were hired for outrageous salaries but little time was spent on building a team. The enormous media attention on the individual personalities of the founders also didn't contribute toward a feeling of belonging.

Competing versus partnerships. Boo.com failed to get trust from enough suppliers, who were reluctant to support a company that worked with their competitors. It failed to see that e-retailing leads to potential channel conflicts which must be managed. The company was dependent on partnerships for its internet platform because it was a relative latecomer in the internet boom, but it was accused of being more deal oriented than partnership oriented, and even seen as specializing in cheating its suppliers.

People centrality versus result centrality. Boo.com's senior management was very demanding of its employees in terms of performance, but they were too busy traveling to do much on the people side of the business. They considered developing employees as a responsibility of the employees themselves and as a consequence Boo.com soon began to struggle to keep its top staff.

Rational versus inspirational. Boo.com's culture aimed at being a "think grand" inspirational culture. Co-founder Malmsten once said: "being an entrepreneur is not about making money; it is about making dreams come true" (Malmsten et al, 2002).

Egalitarian versus hierarchical. Boo.com' s corporate culture was very much a status-oriented one. Being glamorous, wearing fashionable and exclusive clothes, staying in exclusive hotels, and being part of the jet-set were part of it. The company chose a prestigious – and very expensive – location in central London for its headquarters and call center.

Internal drive versus responsiveness. Boo.com spent large amounts of money on online advertising campaigns, while it knew little about the profile of its target group because it failed to analyze the behavior of (potential) customers on the website. And since customer experience drives the success or failure of a site, Boo.com's failed because it ignored the needs of its (potential) customers.

Stable continuity versus dynamic change and *short-term versus long-term orientation*. Boo.com's culture was in line with its ambition to grow the business like a big bang, from start-up to global e-commerce firm at a rapid pace. They needed a lot of starting capital, went for big deals with big partners and became dependent on them. Because the funding was spent on short-term projects, Boo.com was not in the position to start making money when the investors required it to do so.

Start-up companies that do not pay attention to the development of corporate culture easily fall into the trap of becoming extreme on all cultural orientations. This starts to work against the company and ultimately leads to failure. Confidence, internal drive, and individualism need to be balanced with humility and a willingness to listen to the ideas of others in order to create a collaborative culture. Hardly any business leaders manage to make the change from extremely entrepreneurial management in the start-up phase to a management style that fits a more stable corporate culture. One of the exceptions seems to be Dell, the company we will look at next.

Dell

Whizz-kid Michael Dell started his company in 1984, based on the new business idea in the computer industry of bypassing the middleman and selling directly to the consumer (Dell, 1999; Asser and Hampden-Turner, 2001; Park and Burrows, 2003). Now Dell is a Fortune 500 company with 40,000 employees and Michael Dell is still CEO and chairman, until July 2004.

Dell used the start of the downturn in the technology business in 2001 to work on its culture. This has certainly helped it not only to survive the downturn, but also to thrive and become the world's number one PC maker. Dell chose not to respond to the first major restructuring in its history, including the elimination of 6,000 jobs, by focusing even more on financial performance. Instead, it started an initiative called the "Soul of Dell" to change its corporate culture (www.dell.com). This had started off with all the characteristics of an extremely entrepreneurial culture, but analysing Dell's aspired culture makes clear that it was working on reconciling all nine dimensions of corporate culture.

Consistency versus pragmatism. Dell's reconciliation of this dilemma is personified by its two leaders: the entrepreneurial, pragmatic Michael Dell and COO Kevin Rollins (who will be CEO from July 2004), who brought a passion for rigorous measurement and more rigid, long-range planning with him when he joined Dell in 1993 from the consulting business. Through continuously learning from mistakes, Dell implements cost savings and quality improvements. This has made it the champion in manufacturing and distribution efficiency that it now is. The "Soul of Dell" intends to take this reconciling culture a step further. It emphasises that zero tolerance for unethical behavior is a standard for employees as well. The reconciliation here is that Dell does not limit integrity to maintaining legal standards; it has implemented a system of hotlines where anyone worldwide can call anonymously and be connected with an ombudsman to report possible violations of ethics. Dilemmas are then discussed in an ethics committee. Through making everybody responsible for living the value of integrity, the company can learn from these dilemmas and come to consistent policies.

Individualism versus group orientation. Individual accountability and responsibility have always been at the heart of Dell's culture. This dilemma has been reconciled by Dell's "two in a box" principle: two managers share responsibility for a region, product group, or company function, ensuring that they work as a team, combining their individual strengths – Dell and Rollins, who have worked effectively as co-CEOs – set the example at the top level.

Competing versus cooperating. Dell has always been a relentless, competitive machine in its fights with much bigger competitors such as IBM and Compaq. Even although it is now in top position itself, it still instigates price wars as if it were the challenger in the PC market. However it reconciles the dilemma by placing itself strategically in an ecosystem of cooperating players, such as component suppliers. It provides and shares knowledge with partners so that, through its partnerships, it competes in new markets. For instance, it teamed up with EMC on storage equipment, with Lexmark on printers, and with music download company Musicmatch on a portable digital music player.

People centrality versus result centrality. Dell comes from a task/result-oriented corporate culture: a tough, high-pressure environment in which people are expected to deliver and are rewarded for it. One of the triggers of the Soul of Dell initiative was that employee surveys had revealed that Dell staff stayed with the company because it was winning, not because of loyalty. The initiative must make people feel that there is more to the company than just making money by doing a good job. Dell realized that it needed to do more to show appreciation for its people. It had to make the corporate culture more developmental and nurturing instead of a "survival of the fittest" culture. It does so by giving support to the implementation of ideas and business proposals from its people, and by encouraging managers to respond to the need of their staff for work–life balance. The idea is that making people feel that they are citizens of the company will also make them feel just as accountable as its leaders are.

Rational versus inspirational. Michael Dell is a more detached person in comparison with the charismatic leaders of many other 1980s and 90s start-up companies. One of the objectives of the initiative is to make Dell more inspirational. Kevin Rollins frequently mentions George Washington as an example: everybody followed him because he inspired people to do better.

Egalitarian versus hierarchical. Dell's leaders are self-confident business leaders who can come across as autocratic and directive. However, part of the Soul of Dell culture is to maintain a meritocracy and keep on operating without hierarchy and bureaucracy. Dell wants its direct culture to be practiced not just in sales but also in communication. People are encouraged to challenge their bosses; part of culture change is that leadership will listen more and let others participate in decisions.

Internal drive versus responsiveness. The reconciliation of this dilemma is the basis of Dell's success. Through using the internet to give personalized, detailed, information-rich services to its customers, it pushes its direct selling business model to an ever-increasing spectrum of customers. Through being relentlessly responsive to customers' needs, Dell becomes privy to far more information about them and can configure customized packages at highly competitive prices. The reconciliation of this dilemma helped Dell be one of the first companies in its industry to respond to the 2001 downturn; it saw the downturn coming because it was talking to customers on a daily basis. Dell uses this reconciliation in the launch of new products, as well. It connects paying attention to product features and the buying experience to ensuring a fit with its own business model. For instance, when Dell launched its printer product line, it included software to guide customers to Dell's website so that they could order new ink cartridges there.

Dynamic change versus stable continuity. Dell still has the "urgency culture" of a start-up company. It is quick to launch new initiatives but it also does not hesitate to stop these if they do not contribute to profitability and might endanger continuity, as it did with high-end servers and the plan to go into the mobile phone business. Dell practices stable, continuous improvement through the dynamics of experimenting.

Short term versus long term. Dell's corporate culture started off from a fast-paced, short-term-oriented entrepreneurial culture. Dell reconciles the dilemma by demanding that new products are both profitable from day one and contribute to fast growth. Part of the Soul of Dell is to inspire workers to focus on long-term goals, such as participating responsibly in the global marketplace and providing superior shareholder value over time.

Figure 6.2 summarizes how Dell reconciles on all corporate culture

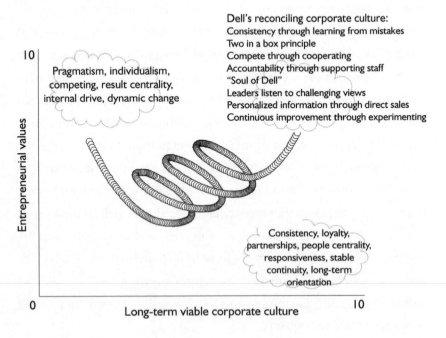

Figure 6.2 Dell corporate culture – reconciling entrepreneurial values with those suitable for a more stable culture

dimensions. Dell is probably the best example of how a start-up company culture can change itself just in time, and establish a reconciling corporate culture for long-term survival.

THE ROLE OF LEADERSHIP IN CHANGING ORGANIZATIONAL CULTURES

As previously mentioned, in companies where the founders are still part of the leadership, the impact of their values is often very clear. The role of leadership is also one of the most critical factors in changing a corporate culture. Their leadership style, communication style, way of handling conflicts, people issues, motivating people, and their attitude to customers have enormous impact on shaping and maintaining a corporate culture. The role of "strong leadership" in creating strong corporate cultures has often been emphasized, but the downside of such leadership is the problem of succession. The choice may seem to be between a guardian of the old culture and finding a new CEO who can drive change. However leaders who create strong cultures often leave little room for the internal development of future leaders who are able to drive change. That makes change of leadership an opportunity as well as a risk for culture change. In a *Harvard Business Review* article published in 2000, Warren Bennis and James O'Toole argued that companies are becoming worse at choosing their bosses and that they should know that internal executives with the potential to be the company's new CEO are not usually apparent. The turnover of CEOs is increasing. Even so, many companies seem to be obsessed by the search for charismatic change leaders from outside instead of developing leadership throughout the organization.

However leaders from outside the company can speed up the process of corporate culture change and there are examples of successful CEOs brought in as external change agents. When success in the past has reinforced a corporate culture to such an extent that it becomes a hindrance for a company to adapt to a changing business environment, appointing a CEO from outside may be necessary. The corporate culture change accomplished by Louis Gerstner at IBM between 1993 and 2002 (described by himself; Gerstner, 2002) shows that an outside leader – he came to IBM without any experience in the computer industry – who pays attention to all corporate culture dimensions in changing from "old" to "new" can be successful. He abolished IBM's "rule by committee" culture, made communication processes more informal, brought in other outsiders at senior management positions, and managed a successful culture change.

In Table 6.1 we have summarized our analysis of how Gerstner addressed all nine corporate culture dimensions in IBM's corporate culture transformation.

However, there are also many examples of leaders appointed from outside who were not successful or had at most a mixed record. Take the appointment in 1999 of Hans Smits as CEO of Rabobank, one of the four biggest banks in the Netherlands, known as a rather conservative organization because of its cooperative structure. Smits seemed to be the right person to change Rabobank's culture in order to make the organization more professional, international, and energetic, within the framework of the consensus-based cooperative structure. He was an outsider without banking experience, but he was an insider in the sense that he had experience in dealing with the Dutch "polder model" (consensus model) as CEO of Schiphol Airport. However after less than three years Smits had to resign because he reportedly "lost the battle against the local bank barons" (NRC Handelsblad, 2002) – he had tried to take away too much of their power.

Table 6.1 Leadership and corporate culture change at IBM

IBM's "old" culture	IBM's "new" culture	Corporate culture dimension
Bureaucracy: Conform to rules and procedures from HQ	Principle driven, able to handle internal complexity and apparent contradiction, and open for diversity	Consistency versus pragmatism
Individualistic: "Not Invented Here," hiding information, internal rivalry	Dedicated individuals working together as a team: sharing information, learning organization, committed to acting as one IBM	Individualism versus group orientation
Act as if there is no competition	Cooperate to compete in providing integrated solutions	Partnership versus competing
Relationship driven "do what you please" culture in which performance did not count	Sensitive to the needs of employees and attention for accountability, discipline in execution and reaching performance objectives	People centrality versus result centrality
Process management "by committee"	Passionate about winning	Rational versus inspirational
Status oriented culture: wait for the boss to decide	Decisiveness by stimulating entrepreneurship throughout the organization	Egalitarian versus hierarchical
"Do it my way" one-sided customer–supplier relationship: next generation product is the starting point	Superior customer service by thinking from the customer's perspective.	Internal drive versus responsiveness
Analysis paralysis	Speed and urgency in execution	Stable continuity versus dynamic change
Conservative	Shareholder value and long-term compelling vision	Short-term versus long-term orientation

Outsiders or insiders?

Collins and Porras, in their 1996 bestseller *Built to Last*, suggest that a change of organization culture requires leaders who combine the more objective view of an outsider with an insider's credibility. These leaders do not necessarily have to come from outside of the organization, they can be leaders from inside who have been in a more peripheral position. The classic example of a "peripheral insider" is Jack Welch. He took over the lead at GE in 1980, coming from the "peripheral" plastics division. Easy said, easy done? Such leaders are notoriously difficult to find.

Most people seem to have forgotten that when, in the late 70s, the GE board was looking for a new CEO, Jack Welch came in at a late stage of the process as a dark horse (Slater, 1993). The risk of appointing outsiders is that they never manage to get inside credibility, as in the example of Smits at Rabobank. The risk of peripheral insiders is that their view is still not objective enough, as is shown in the case of Jan Timmer at Philips Electronics. When he was appointed as CEO of Philips in 1990, he was presented as having inside credibility (because of his lifelong Philips career) and an objective, outsider's view (because he was seen as a divergent element in the Philips culture, a self-made man without a background in technology who had made his name by turnaround operations in Philips divisions). However when his successor Cor Boonstra, who came to Philips after a career at Sara Lee, took over in 1996, he made it clear that Timmer – in his view – had been too much of an insider who had not managed to bring about fundamental change. Boonstra was brought in at Philips because he had a reputation in marketing and because he was known as a leader who was not afraid to take tough, corrective action if financial targets were not met. His first statements as CEO were that Philips needed to get rid of the "bleeders" – a term used by Boonstra to refer to those unprofitable business units which were draining away the profits made by the others – in the organization and that Philips was like a "plate of spaghetti" which needed be transformed into a neat row of asparagus spears. Philips insiders commented at the time that the "neat row of asparagus" was in complete contrast to the traditional Philips idea of synergy in R&D and technology. Interestingly enough, Boonstra was succeeded in 2001 by a genuine insider, Gerard Kleisterlee, who has the more usual background in engineering and has spent his working life at Philips. One of Kleisterlee's actions was to change the composition of the Group Management Committee so that "it can lead across traditional boundaries in our ongoing transformation into one Philips" (www.newscenter.philips.com). The new Philips leadership also openly acknowledges that Boonstra's attempt to put marketing higher up the agenda at Philips has failed. Although Boonstra had succeeded in improving short-term financial results, this leader from the outside had not managed to bring about enduring change.

Hewlett-Packard is another company that chose an outside leader in recent years. The appointment of Carly Fiorina in 1999 was a classic example of appointing an outsider whose personal style ran counter to the existing corporate culture. She was brought in to create a more performance- and service-oriented culture, and – as previously mentioned – decided that the only way was to merge HP with Compaq. The result remains to be seen.

Of course, there are circumstances in which hiring a CEO from outside is the only solution. This can be the case when a corporate culture has become so unhealthy that a newly appointed internal leader would have no credibility. Remember the situation at Ahold which we described earlier? Ahold realized that its culture had become too much of a "follow the leader" one under long-term CEO Cees van der Hoeven. The appointment of an outside CEO with a great track record in the retail industry (former IKEA and Home Depot manager Anders Moberg) was the best choice in that situation, despite the problems it caused. But swinging back and forth between "insiders" and leaders from outside is, in general, not the most effective way of dealing with the paradox of changing organizational culture.

The main issue that causes external change leaders to fail is an underestimation of what is necessary in order to motivate people for enduring corporate culture change. In the different phases of a corporate culture change process, different ways of motivating are crucial. It is useful to look at the impact of two of the corporate culture dimensions on motivation for change:

- People centrality versus result centrality.
- Hierarchical versus egalitarian.

Each quadrant in Figure 6.3 requires a different way of motivating. For enduring change, all four quadrants need to be addressed, although one quadrant may need more attention at a certain stage of the process.

External change agents are often brought in to make organizations which have become complacent more result-oriented and focused on accountability. Therefore most external change agents fit in the quadrant of Result centrality/Egalitarian. They motivate by setting targets and rewarding results – and punishing poor results. Very often they lack the trust which an insider would have, and the insider's credibility in being seen as giving recognition for expert knowledge. The risk is that external change agents will be seen as

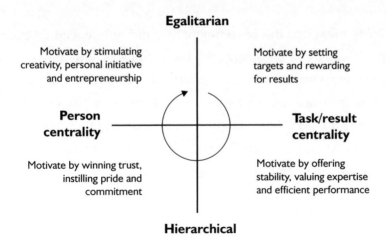

Figure 6.3 Leadership and Corporate Culture change

leaders who "motivate by fear" which will discourage personal initiative and creativity.

Motivating for enduring change can start with setting tough targets, but needs to be combined with giving a clear sense of direction, creating an atmosphere in which people with the right capabilities feel confident that they will be valued, winning their trust and commitment, and giving them the self-respect to take initiatives: a continuous process of using all the four quadrants, as depicted by the circle in Figure 6.3. The motivation repertoire of external change agents may be too limited to accomplish this, resulting in a short shelf-life.

Developing internal change leaders

Ideally, the right person needs to be developed within the organization and there needs to be a pool of talented change agents to choose from in the company itself.

Jim Collins, in his recent bestseller *Good to Great*, found that companies who went through a transformation from being quite ordinary to being great had this in common: they did not depend on charismatic leaders, but on quietly determined bosses, and almost all of them were appointed from inside their organizations. Collins focuses on American companies, but we can recognize his "quietly determined boss" characteristic in some European leaders as well: Jorma Ollila of Nokia and Peter Elverding of Dutch chemical company DSM, for example.

However it seems to be difficult to develop leaders who can act as fundamental change agents from within the organization. We believe that the tendency to equate value-driven organizations with a rigid translation of core values to leadership competencies and preferred behaviors plays an important role here. Assessment based on competencies that are deeply embedded in the existing culture will lead to what has been called "cultural lock-in" and will make it difficult to find leaders who can change the organization from within. An organization that tells its people what the common personal characteristics to be found in business leaders are (and even teaches them what behaviors are good and bad) will produce clones or cynics, especially when competencies and behaviors are formulated as "show determination to achieve excellent results" and "find better ways."

The focus in formulating leadership competencies should be on what is necessary for the future of the company. One way to develop change leaders is to stimulate dissent and listen to it. Nokia uses several tools to encourage open discussion and debate (see www.nokia.com). It has a globally conducted "listening to you" employee survey and an "ask HR" feedback channel on its HR Intranet, where every employee can comment or ask questions about Nokia's people practices and processes, also anonymously, and receive a prompt and openly published response. We do not

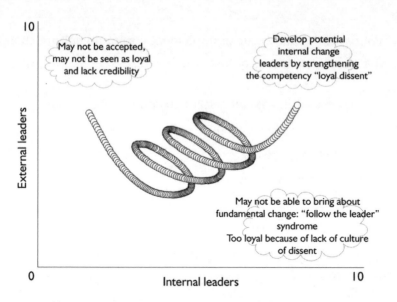

Figure 6.4 Successful change leadership – the dilemma between change leaders from outside or inside the organization

mean to say that provoking dissent is the ultimate solution for developing change leaders. We started this chapter with saying that continuity and change need to be reconciled. The reconciliation is as suggested in Figure 6.4: strengthen the loyal dissent competency in order to develop potential internal change agents.

TRANSFORMING CORPORATE CULTURES AS PART OF STRATEGIC CHANGE PROCESSES

The anthropologist Paul Bohannan once said: "Cultures are adaptive – until the context changes so that it is no longer adaptive" (Bohannan, 1995). This holds for corporate cultures as well. The characteristics of a culture that made it successful are reinforced over time. When the business environment changes, it then becomes very difficult to change such a corporate culture and corporate culture can even become a hindrance to a company's adaptation. This is why most companies wait to implement corporate culture change until a crisis occurs, one for instance due to:

- changes in the market and/or customer expectations
- pressures of globalization
- competitor pressure
- new technology/new products
- a merger or acquisition
- damage to company reputation
- lack of ability to keep top people and/or high potentials on board.

Companies that have used a crisis as a trigger to start a major corporate culture transformation include Lego (response to upcoming multimedia technology), Shell (response to damaged corporate reputation – the Brent Spar affair), Philips (response to lack of competitiveness revealed by competitor pressure and pressure of globalization) and Siemens, the German electronics conglomerate.

Siemens is arguably Europe's strongest conglomerate with a global presence, with some 450,000 employees and with a long history: it was responsible for several technological breakthroughs as far back as the nineteenth century. Siemens CEO Heinrich von Pierer promised corporate culture change to the stock market in 1998, when the company was in crisis (Ewing, 2000). The change process is still ongoing (Boston and Kempe, 2001; Business Week, 2002; Economist, 2003) but when we look at the results to date we can recognize that Siemens has worked on a corporate culture change on all nine corporate culture dimensions. They are illustrated in Figure 6.5; let's run through them here:

- From a culture characterized by bureaucracy and systemic

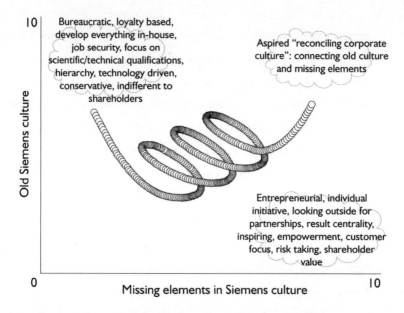

Figure 6.5 Corporate culture revitalization process at Siemens

control to an entrepreneurial culture, both in Germany and worldwide.

• From a culture where loyalty comes first to a culture in which people freely express their individual opinions and take initiatives. Actually, when Von Pierer criticized Siemens' culture in 1998, it came as a big culture shock; criticizing the corporate culture of his own company in public was not something that a loyal, experienced CEO of a company such as Siemens was expected to do.

• From a culture of developing everything in-house to a culture of looking outside for partnerships. At the end of the 90s, Siemens still planned to build an internet venture in-house but from 2000 onward it increased its internet presence via strategic alliances. In its computer operations it signed a worldwide cooperation pact with Fujitsu as part of the strategy to compete more aggressively.

- From a people-oriented culture with a high emphasis on job security to a more cost- and result-oriented culture. Compensation tied to incentives based upon business and financial performance is now normal practice at Siemens, but Siemens did not copy the hire-and-fire US model. Siemens uses the strengths of the people-oriented side of its culture, for example the system of codetermination which requires sharing strategy with works council representatives and the fact that labor unions have seats on supervisory boards, in order to develop better measures for cost effectiveness and to codevelop ideas for new business with labor representatives.

- From a rational culture with a focus on scientific and technical qualifications to a culture in which social skills, including the ability to motivate people in a more creative way and to work in an international environment, are valued more highly.

- From a culture with a clear hierarchical structure and pay increase/promotion based on seniority to a culture in which employees are empowered and evaluate their managers.

- From an engineering culture, with an internal focus on processes and systems, to a culture more focused on the customer and the image of the brand.

- From a stable, conservative, risk-avoiding culture to an innovation-based culture, a "global network of innovation." Siemens is now one of the most R&D-intensive companies in the world and has introduced elements in its culture to encourage people to capture and incorporate new ideas to show a more dynamic and innovative image to the customer (Von Pierer and Van Oetinger, 2001). The speed of bringing new products to the market has increased enormously.

- From a culture of indifference to shareholders to a balance between focus on shareholder value and the interests of other stakeholders.

Just as corporate cultures are not formed in one day, corporate culture change may require several years, as in the Siemens example. The Siemens case also shows clearly that corporate culture change is about changing systems, structures, and processes, but is in the end also about changing people. Corporate culture change requires every employee from the CEO to the most junior member of staff to change their ways of thinking and behaving.

APPROACH TO CORPORATE CULTURE CHANGE

The rationale for corporate culture change can be very different. The main reasons to embark on a corporate culture change process are among the following:

- Revitalizing the corporate culture after downsizing.
- Restructuring in relation to a crisis.
- In relation to strategic change processes such as globalization, or after making some major acquisitions in different parts of the world.
- Moving to a different technology or core business.
- In reaction to changing attitudes to work.

Despite these differences in the reasons for starting corporate culture change, there are similarities in the approach to the process of corporate culture transformation (as discussed in Chapter 1):

- The process must address the dilemma between preserving tradition and fostering innovation: "continuity through renewal."
- It must be a process of constructive confrontation involving all stakeholders.

- The process must explicitly address the tension and find the balance between seemingly contradicting values.
- The process must provide an opportunity to discuss the dilemmas people face in day-to-day practices.

We will now introduce our approach to corporate culture change, focusing on corporate culture transformation that inevitably goes together with strategic change processes such as globalization.

Outline for corporate culture change process

Let's take as a starting point a situation in which a company has defined a new envisioned future and strategy, so that it is important to understand to what extent the existing corporate culture supports attaining the envisioned future and strategic objectives, and to what extent it hinders attaining them. This can be the base of a corporate culture change process that not just supports but even drives the process of attaining the strategic objectives and making the envisioned future real. The first stage of the process is an assessment of the current corporate culture and the desired corporate culture, including an analysis of the gap between them.

The process of defining the future, desired corporate culture is not a matter of sending the board for a two-day, off-site workshop to determine new "core values" and then sticking these up all over the place in the company. Defining new core values and putting them on posters and in brochures without a process of involving the whole company inevitably makes the values the subject of jokes and laughter. For example, days after one company had defined "the winning spirit" as a new core value, its employees had invented a cartoon character – "the spinning whirrit" – which mocked the whole process. There is more to corporate culture than just core values and, moreover, culture change needs to start by assessing what your current corporate culture is before even thinking about where you want to be. Assessment of the existing culture, reflected in the values of people, but also in the systems, processes, and structures of the company, as well as in daily behaviors and practices, is not an easy step. We've seen all too often that the assessment of the current corporate culture at board level leads to a different result than an assessment by middle management, young high potentials, or members of the works council. Part of a culture assessment is about confronting management with different perceptions about what their company is really like.

Figure 6.6 gives an outline of the approach to facilitate corporate culture change. We will go through the different steps in this outline in the remaining part of the chapter.

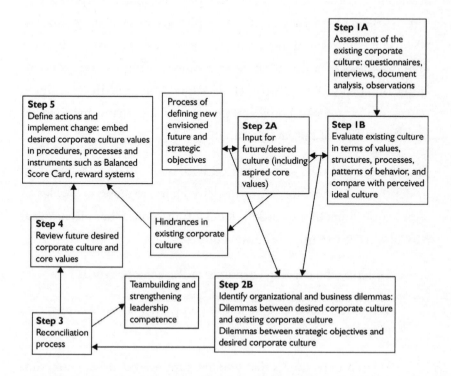

Figure 6.6 Outline of corporate culture change process

Step 1: Assessment of current corporate culture

An assessment using a questionnaire that provides a quantitative comparison between the current and the ideal culture helps to trigger the discussion. Most managers like quantitative data. In our approach at THT we prefer to accompany quantitative data with a qualitative assessment of the corporate culture, based on document analysis, web-based questionnaires with open questions, in-depth, face-to-face interviews, focus groups, storytelling, and observations. We have spent time talking to customers on the shop floor of a retail company and have attended management team meetings as observers in order to assess corporate cultures. The outcome of the process may be confrontational for top managers because it might show that the problems are at their level. What top managers preach is not always in accordance with what they practice. Such a corporate culture assessment is a good start to a corporate culture change process, because it is the beginning of a learning process. Figures 6.7 and 6.8 give examples of a quantitative assessment using the nine dimensions of corporate culture. They show that middle managers perceive a larger gap between current and ideal cultures than do board members of the same company.

The quantitative data are supported with qualitative data, based on in-depth interviews, focus groups, etc. Here are some examples of simple questions that we ask in focus groups, ones that often reveal a lot about the existing corporate culture:

1. Describe the existing corporate culture in one word.

2. What do you have to do in this company to make a career, e.g., be promoted, be rewarded?

3. What are the things that you are supposed to do in your company, though you won't be penalized if you ignore them?

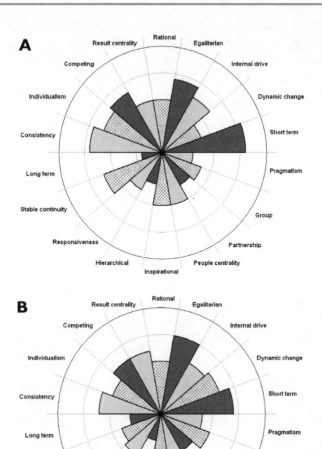

Figure 6.7 Corporate culture profile – evaluation by top management. (A) Evaluation of existing corporate culture; (B) perceived ideal corporate culture

4. What should you avoid doing because it would hurt your career?

5. Characterize your company culture in terms of a car, a TV personality, an animal, a musical instrument, etc., including the associations that you have.

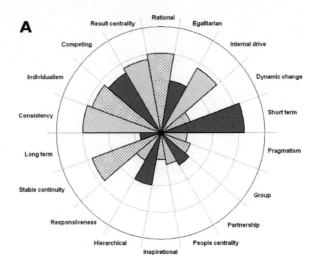

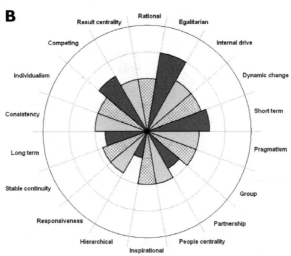

Figure 6.8 Corporate culture profile – evaluation by middle management. (A) Evaluation of existing corporate culture; (B) perceived ideal corporate culture

6.   What binds the people in your company, what makes you proud of your company in the current situation? (It often turns out that this question is difficult to answer. "Proud to be innovative" frequently comes up in technology-oriented companies.

7.   What separates people, what keeps people apart in your company?

8.   What are the hindrances in your corporate culture for future success? (This question often brings "quick wins" because it leads to direct actions for removing hindrances in the existing corporate culture, such as organizational structures that hinder customer orientation, overflow of corporate initiatives, etc.)

Here are some examples of responses from one company to Question 2: What do you have to do in this company to make a career, e.g., be promoted, be rewarded?

Listen to your boss.

Follow the rules.

Be loyal.

Network with successful people.

Get to know key decision makers well.

Understand the politics and play the political games.

Show creativeness.

Make sure that you're seen/noticed.

Travel frequently.

Be able to express yourself.

Show concrete results soon.

Make profit.

Achieve given targets.

Maintain your professional attitude.

Put your working life before anything else, work hard.

Be honest.

Make sure that you are responsible for prestigious customers.

Of course, what is not mentioned in response to this question is also relevant.

Here are some examples of responses from one company to Question 3: What are the things that you are supposed to do in your company, though you won't be penalized if you ignore them?

Being open and expressing strong views.

Taking decisions.

Documenting your work.

Serving customers.

Understanding customers.

Empowering and coaching your people.

Committing yourself to all company initiatives.

Focus on corporate success rather than own success.

Sharing knowledge.

Taking risks.

Being open about your mistakes.

Meeting commitments to colleagues.

Here are some examples of responses from one company to Question 4: What should you avoid doing because it would hurt your career?

Be disloyal to your boss.

Disagree publicly with big bosses.

Showing disrespect and lack of understanding of the history of the company.

Be too "innovative."

Reveal others' mistakes.

Be dishonest.

Forget the customer.

Fail to achieve certain targets.

Challenge decisions.

Be unconventional in behavior, dress, hairstyle.

In our web-based questionnaires we ask open questions about organization structure, decision making, leadership, human resource management issues, communication processes, customer relationships, etc. We also try to elicit key dilemmas in the corporate culture by asking respondents to describe tensions they face that can be described in the format: On the one hand… versus on the other hand… This turns out to be a very effective of getting a first impression of the dilemmas between the existing culture and the ideal culture, such as in the following example:

On the one hand…	Whilst on the other hand…
"One company" implies treating employees the same in all locations	Differences in history and labor market mean that people are treated differently

Step 1 in the corporate culture change process serves two purposes. The first is in raising the awareness about the change process itself. Some of the hindrances in the existing culture (e.g., those that come up in response to Question 8) can be translated into direct actions to take away the hindrances. Secondly, it gives input for a discussion at executive management level. The combination of results from the quantitative tools, in-depth interviews, etc., leads to a good picture of how the existing corporate culture is perceived, what the perceived ideal culture is, and what the hindrances and dilemmas are.

Step 2: Desired corporate culture

The assessment of the existing and ideal culture can then be used as input for an executive management workshop and serves as a tool to raise awareness of the current corporate culture and to trigger the discussion. In addition to going through a similar exercise as described in Step 1, the following questions are discussed:

1. *What needs to be the focus for making the envisioned future/strategy work?* The objective of corporate culture change is not to completely reject the existing culture and change it to the "ideal" culture, with the risk of throwing away the best of the existing culture. The focus of the discussion is then this: what do we need to retain, and what do we need to change in order to be successful in the future?

2. *Which values are already present but should be strengthened in order not to throw away the strengths of the current culture?* For instance, one company in the food industry decided that its strong points of quality consciousness, technology orientation, and cost leadership orientation should be retained and strengthened.

3. *Which values are currently scarcely present, but should be developed because they are desired to make the envisioned future and strategy work?* As an example, the same food-industry company decided that "openness in communication" and "personal initiative" were lacking and needed to be part of the desired culture. Here are some other examples of responses on this question:

Long-term thinking.
Reacting quickly in the context of strategy.
Open discussions.
Open mind, understanding customer needs.
Know the organization better (e.g., management should know the high potentials).
Continuous learning about what the customer wants.
Cooperation between different units.

At this stage of the process we revisit the dilemmas between the existing and ideal cultures and repeat the "on the one hand…versus on the other hand…" exercise. This is in order to reveal the tensions between the existing corporate culture and the desired one, and the tensions between the envisioned future and strategy and the desired corporate culture (Step 2B in Figure 6.6).

Corporate culture profiles such as the ones in Figures 6.7 and 6.8 give a quantitative input of the main tensions on the nine corporate culture dimensions, which helps in structuring the qualitative output of the workshops. In our experience at THT, the main tensions that come out of the qualitative analysis of existing and desired culture can almost invariably be mapped on these nine dimensions as well.

Here are some examples of tensions between desired and existing corporate culture and between desired corporate culture and envisioned future/strategy, including the corporate culture dimension associated with each tension.

Desired corporate culture	versus	Existing corporate culture
Systems, projects, and objectives across locations	versus	Local entrepreneurship: ad-hoc local initiatives
Consistency		Pragmatism

Envisioned future and strategy	versus	Desired corporate culture
We have to reassess whether an employee still adds high value frequently	versus	We try to build loyalty and commitment among employees
Individualism		Group orientation

Envisioned future and strategy	versus	Desired corporate culture
We are supposed to start sharing R&D with our competitors and release information about unique innovations	versus	We need to be aggressively competitive to survive cut-throat competition in our fast changing markets
Partnership orientation		Competing

Desired corporate culture	versus	Envisioned future and strategy
We need to give people room for personal development	versus	We need to take quick decisions to have commercial success
People centrality		Result centrality

Desired corporate culture	versus	Existing corporate culture
We want to be a leader in corporate responsibility issues	versus	We want to keep business volume and profit up
Inspirational		Rational

Desired corporate culture	versus	Existing corporate culture
Maximal internal and external openness and transparency	versus	Control of information flow
Egalitarian		Hierarchical

Desired corporate culture	versus	Existing corporate culture
We want to be customer-driven according to concepts such as relationship management and bundled buying	versus	Customers are buying the best product available in the market without consideration to the relationship
Responsiveness		Internal drive

Desired corporate culture	versus	Existing corporate culture
We put all our resources in high risk new product/service development	versus	Clients expect us to deliver the products we are traditionally strong in
Dynamic change		Stable continuity

Envisioned future and strategy	versus	Desired corporate culture
Shareholder value	versus	Stakeholder value
Short-term orientation		Long-term orientation

At this point the group is in the position to make a first draft of core values that will serve as an anchor for the corporate culture change process. Corporate culture core values need to address the tension between existing culture, desired culture, and envisioned future. The answers on Step 2's Questions 2 and 3 (which values should be strengthened, which values should be further developed) and the tensions such as the ones listed above give sufficient input to come up with a draft list of the four or five most important values that will differentiate the company culture from others.

For instance, the company in the food industry that wanted to retain quality consciousness, technology orientation, and cost leadership, and that wanted to develop openness and individual initiative, came up with core values such as:

- Striving for continuous improvement (in order to retain quality, technology, and cost leadership orientation).
- Openness.
- Fostering intrapreneurship (stimulating individual initiative).

Step 3: The reconciliation process – discussion and dilemma reconciliation in focus groups and intact teams (incorporating Steps 4 and 5)

At this stage a process is started at different locations involving different levels in the organization to discuss the desired corporate culture, draft core values, and to review and reconcile the organizational and business dilemmas in order to "live" the values. This can be done in focus groups brought together for this purpose or in intact management teams that relate the discussion to their own issues.

The focus groups or teams go through the following process:

- Objectives of the corporate culture change process.
- The business case: benefits of the corporate culture change process and implementing new core values; effect of not implementing the values.
- What people miss in the desired corporate culture and the target values. Per target value, the focus groups discuss:
  – Behaviors that demonstrate this value.
  – Behaviors that undermine this value.
  – What are the obstacles and dilemmas to live this value?

– What needs to be done to live this value (the reconciliation process)?

– How are we going to measure that we live this value?

This process is not just a step in the corporate culture change program, it serves at the same time as a leadership competence development, because the reconciliation process helps to develop a crucial competence. The focus groups/teams also give useful input for translating each of the values into behaviors to be treasured and promoted in order to live the value, and into behaviors to reject and fight in order to do the same.

On the basis of the results from the focus groups, the desired corporate culture and target values are reviewed (shown as Step 4 in the process of Figure 6.6). If necessary, changes and additions are made, followed by the implementation of action plans for change (shown as Step 5 in the process of Figure 6.6).

As examples of how participants in the process work on dilemma reconciliation, let's look at two of the tensions mentioned in Step 2: People centrality versus result centrality and internal drive versus responsiveness.

Commercial success (result centrality) versus mentoring people (people centrality)

On the one hand, a company needs to achieve commercial success with clients and suppliers. Satisfied, long-term clients are the ultimate test of contribution. On the other hand, mentoring – managing and developing colleagues and subordinates – ultimately accelerates their development and benefits the firm. This dilemma is illustrated in Figure 6.9.

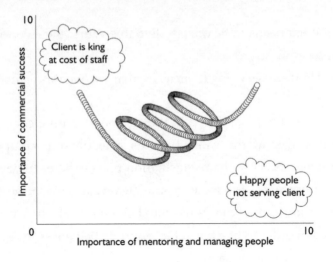

Figure 6.9 The commercial success versus mentoring people dilemma

The following scorecard is used to evaluate where the corporate culture stands now and where it needs to move. We ask: Where would you locate your organization? (Place an X). Where would you like to see it move? (Place an O). What organizational measures can the firm implement to move closer to the 10/10 position?

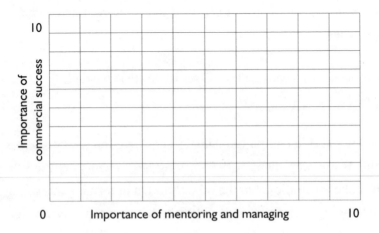

Reliable technology (internal drive) versus customer orientation (responsiveness)

This tension represents the dilemma concerning the coordination between efficient technology and customer orientation. This is a manifestation of the dilemma between internal drive (leading to a focus on the internal organization including its efficient and reliable technology) versus responsiveness (leading to the need to be constantly informed by important customers about their needs and demands for new technologies) and is depicted in Figure 6.10.

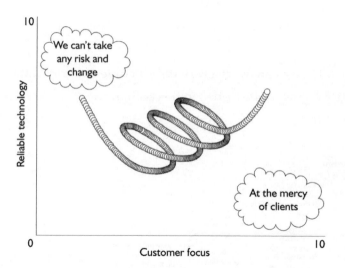

Figure 6.10   Internal organization versus customer orientation

The following scorecard is used to evaluate where the corporate culture stands now and where it needs to move. We ask: Where would you locate your organization? (Place an X). Where would you like to see it move? (Place an O). What organizational measures can the company implement to move closer to the 10/10 position?

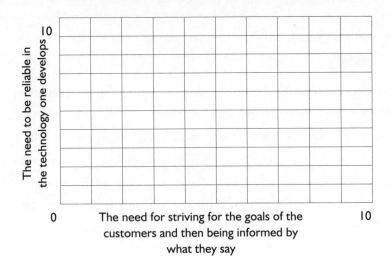

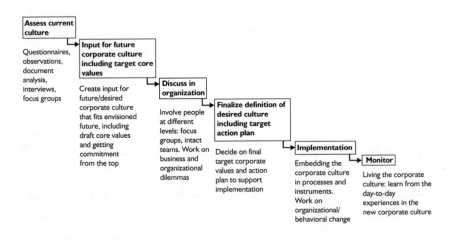

Figure 6.11 gives an overview of the schedule of a corporate culture change program as described in this section.

Figure 6.11   Corporate culture change program

DEALING WITH RESISTANCE TO CHANGE

It is the nature of man as he grows older, to protest against change, particularly change for the better.
John Steinbeck, *Travels with Charley: In Search of America*

One of the most frequent mistakes made in corporate culture change programs is to label those who resist change as "negative." Change seen as positive by leadership is not necessarily seen as good by everybody, and they may have good reasons for their reactions. Organizational life is always more complex than it looks from above. Corporate cultures are living systems and not as malleable as a product. Those who actively resist are more likely to cooperate in the end than those who avoid confrontation and remain passive. The main dilemma in dealing with the human elements of changing a corporate culture is therefore between focus on the hard issues (often leading to a "bone-breaking approach" in corporate culture change, which will only increase resistance) versus focus on the "soft issues" – ensuring that employees are connected and motivated to give of their best.

An important lesson of corporate culture change is that the existing corporate culture itself determines what kind of change will be accepted. In a culture where change is seen as something you only do when you are desperate, culture change will be resisted by people who have an interest in maintaining the status quo. In a culture where change is seen as a way of life, conflicts in culture change will be openly handled and resolved. In stable continuity cultures, change will be more accepted when it is evolutionary and planned. In dynamic change cultures, revolutionary change is acceptable. In egalitarian cultures, everybody needs to be involved in the process and be allowed to express their opinion. In hierarchical cultures, driving the change process from the top is more acceptable.

The concept of the reconciling corporate culture helps in making change more acceptable, because it is based on the premise that change and continuity need to be reconciled. It helps to convince people that change is necessary to preserve what is most valuable to them, such as innovative capability, close customer contact, informality, or open communication.

In summary, here are some of the lessons we have learned in corporate culture change processes that help in getting commitment throughout the organization:

- Know where you start from: study the existing culture and its strengths/weaknesses.
- Use the reconciling corporate culture concept to explain that change is a process of "continuity through renewal."
- Involve people in the process: discuss real dilemmas, challenges, and hindrances.
- Delegate responsibility and empower people to implement concrete change.
- Over-communication is better than under-communication in a corporate culture change process.
- Define project roles: sponsors, "culture change" agents, facilitators.
- Make the corporate culture change process part of existing organizational programs.
- Work on profound change (at the level of basic assumptions and core values) and on making organizational and behavioral changes to bring the desired culture to life.
- Make sure that high-level executives walk the talk as well.

- A meaningful set of corporate values is a mix of existing core values and new, aspirational values.
- Culture change is about managing tension:
  - Between old and new, change and continuity
  - Between global and local
  - Between results focus and people focus.

Integrating different corporate cultures in mergers, acquisitions, joint ventures, and alliances

n preparing for mergers, acquisitions, joint ventures, and alliances, the emphasis is often on financial, legal, and technical matters. The cultural factor is often neglected. However, nearly every day the financial press reports on international mergers, acquisitions, and other forms of strategic alliances that face problems caused by differences in corporate culture. Well-known examples include the DaimlerChrysler "merger," the failed Dutch–Italian alliance between KLM and Alitalia, Corus (the merger of British Steel and Dutch Hoogovens) and the merger between AOL and Time Warner, where the creative e-culture seems to have lost out and the old media culture become dominant over time.

This chapter discusses how different corporate cultures can be successfully integrated in post-merger, post-acquisition, joint venture, and strategic alliance processes. All companies involved in integration processes face the dilemma between the complete integration of corporate cultures versus allowing for differentiation. Integration processes very often result in the domination of one corporate culture, instead of in the creation of a reconciling culture. We will show that creating a reconciling culture is more likely to ensure successful mergers, acquisitions, joint ventures, and alliances.

A recent KPMG study identified the most common causes of cross-border alliance failures. Relational aspects like cultural differences and lack of trust turned out to be responsible for 70 percent of alliance failures. This is even more striking when we realize that building trust is a cultural challenge in itself. Lack of trust is often caused by different views of what constitutes a trustworthy partner. Is a trustworthy partner one who works according to consistent management processes or is a trustworthy partner one who is willing to be pragmatic and to make exceptions because of the good business relationship? As discussed in Chapter 2, corporate cultures

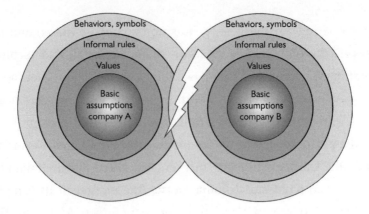

Figure 7.1   When two cultures collide

differ in the specific solutions they choose for universally shared human problems, which often present themselves in the form of dilemmas. Consistency versus flexibility is just one of the cultural dilemmas that frequently occurs in cross-border cooperation (Figure 7.1).

This does not mean that cultural differences cannot be overcome, but it does mean that it is essential not to ignore cultural differences. For example, the mistake made at the initial stages of the merger between Daimler and Chrysler was that everyone assumed that cultural difference would be resolved by itself. Jurgen Schrempp, Daimler's CEO, described the merger with Chrysler as a "marriage made in heaven." Despite this, it would later become apparent that corporate cultural differences were a main stumbling block.

CULTURAL DUE DILIGENCE

One of the main reasons that culture is often neglected in post-merger integration processes is that it is seen as intangible and management is more comfortable with hard figures. It is, however, possible to make cultural differences tangible using a process that explores and identifies the differences, potential challenges, and areas of synergy of the partners in the merger and acquisition. Next, using a structured process, the partners learn to reconcile the differences in such a way that seemingly opposing cultural orientations are integrated on a higher level. This methodology that we use at THT for integrating corporate cultures is cultural due diligence, as part of an overall due diligence process. In a cultural due diligence process we map the cultural similarities and differences existing between the prospective partners in a merger or acquisition, using questionnaires, interviews, observations, and focus groups. Next, we identify the most important potential dilemmas and opportunities for integrating diversity, both in terms of people and systems. Thereafter the reconciliation approach is used to connect seemingly opposing cultural orientations and ways of working in the context of realizing business results.

The three-step approach

The nine dimensions of corporate culture model provide a framework for identifying and understanding the corporate culture differences and their underlying logics. In an international merger, acquisition, or joint venture, the corporate culture differences will be partly related to national cultural differences, making the integration process even more complicated. Making mergers and acquisitions successful requires a three-step approach:

1.   Awareness

2.   Respect

3.   Resolving dilemmas: the process of reconciliation

Awareness

A "cultural gap analysis" of corporate cultural differences is only a first step in raising awareness of the differences. To what extent cultural differences become problematic in an organizational integration process depends on the relationship between the parties in the mergers and acquisitions process. What are the perceptions of the parties about each other, which party is in a more powerful position, how do the two parties handle the cultural and power differences? It is important not just to map the differences, but also to assess how the companies and their leaders deal with the differences. In practice, the major origin of cultural differences between an organization and a new partner may lie in one or two cultural dimensions.

For instance, one of the questions in our questionnaire asks people to choose between the following two descriptions of the essence of an organization:

> *"An organization is a system designed to perform functions and tasks in an efficient way."*

> *"An organization is a group of people working together; the functioning of the company depends on the social relationships between the people and the relationships with the organization."*

This question is one of the measurements of the people centrality versus result centrality dimension of our corporate culture model. The corporate cultures of American companies tend to put a higher value on result centrality: the system can be perceived as disassociated from the people. The corporate cultures of Southern European and Asian companies tend to value people centrality more.

It is clear that, if these types of differences are not recognised, problems between – for instance – an American and a French company involved in an integration process are almost certain to occur. Cultural differences will cause people to work and communicate differently, choose different solutions, formulate different objectives, develop different strategies. All of this will eventually lead to conflicts after the merger or acquisition has taken place if these differences are not fully recognized and respected.

Respect

The second step, respecting differences, starts with realising the limitations of your own corporate culture orientation and the positive aspects of the contrasting orientation. An American company should, for instance, realise that the extreme of viewing a company as a system leads to an organization in which all human resources are reengineered out of the organization. On the other hand, a Japanese company needs to realise that the extreme manifestation of a people centrality corporate culture will lead to camouflaging weaknesses and mistakes out of loyalty to other members of the organization. The step of respect for cultural differences is particularly important, since a lack of respect often causes distrust between different cultures. The lack of respect has the effect of perceiving the partner's cultural orientation not so much as being "different" but as being "wrong."

By naming positive and negative aspects of both orientations, the dilemmas will automatically emerge. Thereafter one can conduct an analysis of those dilemmas that will constitute the biggest risks/ challenges.

Reconciliation

The third step is reconciliation: resolving the dilemmas by connecting the different corporate culture values in such a manner that they work with each other in a mutually enhancing way. The reconciliation approach helps the companies involved to see and understand how alternative perspectives can help their own and actually enrich each other. If you are global, you need to be sensitive to local conditions. If the strength of an organization is individual creativity, it needs teams to make that into an innovation. If your corporate culture tends to push new technology, you need to know what market you want to be pulled by in order to be responsive to your customers.

It is not self-evident that managers will choose a reconciliation strategy when involved in a merger, acquisition, or alliance. Reconciliation requires intercultural competence – the ability to look at the world from various different perspectives and to reconcile those perspectives. Furthermore, management of both parties to a merger or acquisition process are not always motivated to reconcile. In practice we often see that management chooses other strategies than reconciliation, depending on the corporate cultures concerned, the context in which the deal was made, and the relationship between the partners. How big the measurable differences in corporate culture are is often irrelevant. The extent to which cultural differences become problematical in an organizational integration process is dependent on things like these: What are the partner's mutual perceptions of each other, which party is the most powerful, how do both parties handle the cultural differences?

DIFFERENT STRATEGIES

In our consulting practice we encounter different strategies for dealing with corporate culture differences. Those that we encounter include the dominating strategy (a "roll over approach" by the most powerful party), leading to a defensive strategy from the partner (actively resisting domination by the other party); the tolerating strategy (keeping the partner at arm's length) and the "avoidance" strategy (ignoring the differences). These strategies are often ineffective in making mergers and acquisitions successful.

The dominating strategy, the defensive strategy, and the avoidance strategy all have one thing in common: a lack of respect for other cultural orientations. If there is no respect for the partner then a reconciliation strategy will be impossible.

Figure 7.2 illustrates the different possible strategies for dealing with cultural differences, including a possible reconciliation strategy. In the dominating strategy, the party with the most power tries to force

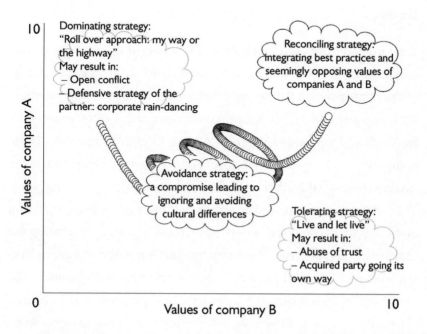

Figure 7.2   Different strategies in mergers and acquisitions

its partner to accept its way of doing things and its culture. This attitude of "my way or the highway" forces the least powerful partner to use a defensive strategy – to use active resistance against the dominant party in order to preserve its culture and its own way of doing things. In some cases this can lead to failure of the merger at an early stage, as happened in June 2001 when Alcatel attempted to impose a dominance strategy on Lucent during negotiations. Sometimes, as in the DaimlerChrysler situation, the partner is so weak that it has no choice but to go along with the merger. That may lead to corporate rain-dancing: the less dominant party joins the dance, but has its own agenda for preserving control and its own culture. The example of Chrysler shows that this is not very effective. At the start of the cooperation possible cultural differences were wilfully ignored in order to avoid discussions and confrontations (avoidance strategy). However, members of both organizations were soon confronted with the differences, and with Daimler's dominating strategy.

The "merger" between Daimler and Chrysler is an example of two corporate cultures that are both unwilling to accept the dominance of the other partner. Companies that are more partnership oriented, such as many Dutch and Scandinavian companies, often grant more freedom and autonomy when acquiring foreign companies. These companies are often rather reserved in using power and more inclined to leave the other company with its freedom and autonomy. They often choose a tolerating strategy – "live and let live" or "living apart together" – keeping a partner at a distance and postponing the real integration process. This happened at Corus (the merger of British Steel and Dutch Hoogovens). For a long time both partners did just that, kept each other at a distance and postponed the cultural integration process. However, when tough decisions needed to be made, such as about the proposed sale of Corus' aluminium division, cultural differences led to a standoff between the Dutch and the British side. British management was not prepared for differences in the culture of corporate governance between the UK and continental Europe. In the Dutch system, power is distributed more equally and the Supervisory Board of Corus Netherlands decided to do what it saw as its responsibility, and blocked the proposed sale, leading to the resignation of the British CEO.

The avoidance strategy is a compromise leading to avoiding and ignoring value dilemmas. That is what happened when Dutch IT company Getronics acquired Wang Global in 1999 – without much success, in view of the resignation of Getronics' CEO Cees van Luijk in June 2001.

The helix in Figure 7.2 symbolizes the process of reconciling opposing orientations: the reconciliation strategy. The purpose of this strategy is to find solutions in the top right hand corner of the diagram (10,10); solutions that increase the impact of cultural values through connecting with other values.

The awareness of cultural differences does not guarantee that the integration process will be successful. The second step of the due diligence process, respect for differences, is just as important. Respect for cultural differences should bring about acceptance of the fact that others have a right to interpret the world in their own way. What are the limitations of your own cultural orientation, what are the strengths of their cultures? More and more we find proof that in mergers and acquisitions value is created by the reconciliation strategy of integrating seemingly opposing values.

Reconciling strategy: Borealis

The acquisition of the Austrian company PCD by the petrochemical company Borealis, based in Denmark, is a case in point. Borealis did make an effort to connect the different corporate culture orientations of the two companies in such a way that they could work together. Although Borealis was the acquiring party, it treated its partner as an equal.

The differences in corporate cultures between Borealis and PCD were quite large. Borealis, formed in 1994 by a merger of the petrochemical activities of Norwegian Statoil and Finnish Neste combined many corporate culture characteristics that are typically found in Northern European companies: decentralized, people oriented, informal, egalitarian, consensus oriented, open, and with a very constructive relationship between management and workers' representatives. PCD had a corporate culture typical of a mid-sized Austrian company: a more hierarchical, more decisive, more result oriented, and more formal corporate culture. Both parties were afraid that the post-acquisition integration process would lead to each losing the strengths of its own culture. PCD was afraid of losing the ability to react quickly to market situations. Borealis was afraid that it would lose openness, directness, and people centrality. Even so, the acquiring party Borealis decided not to opt for a dominating or tolerating strategy, but decided to open up to the corporate culture of its partner. Borealis allowed PCD to be involved in the design for restructuring the company even before the acquisition was completed. Moreover, Borealis initiated a transparent, externally facilitated, assessment process for all management levels, thereby ensuring that managers would be selected only on their professional skills, and not on nationality. Clear criteria were formulated for important decisions such as selection of IT systems and the closure of offices which would become redundant because of the integration of activities. The whole process took 18 months. It resulted in a corporate culture for the combined company which reconciled the main differences. By involving many people in the decision making process, making quick decisions became acceptable. By taking personal circumstances of people into account, people committed themselves to stretched performance targets. Through being approachable as management, a hands-on focus was ensured.

MAIN CORPORATE CULTURE DILEMMAS

We have discussed a number of dilemmas that occur during cross-border mergers and acquisitions. In general, differences on all nine dimensions of corporate culture may show up in the form of dilemmas in integration processes:

- Regarding the structure and processes of the organization: centralized systems versus decentralization and acceptance of diversity in strategy and practices.

- Reward systems: rewarding individual performance versus rewarding team achievements.

- Attitude towards the partner: trying to dominate versus a co-operative approach in which each party is willing to adapt to the other.

- People management: focus on people development issues versus focus on performance and pay issues.

- Leadership: low-key styles versus visionary leadership.

- Decision making and communication: an egalitarian, consensus-oriented style with open communication versus a style more used to accepting hierarchy, status, and directive decision making.

- Concept of customer service: different levels of customer intimacy.

- Attitude to change: evolutionary versus revolutionary change.

- Planning: short-term shareholder value focus versus long-term planning and innovation.

We will continue this chapter with a discussion of three corporate culture integration cases in more detail.

The case of Daimler Chrysler

The merger between Daimler-Benz and Chrysler is one of the most prominent recent cross-border mergers. When the companies announced their intention to merge in 1998, the two CEOs, Jurgen Schrempp (Daimler Benz) and Bob Eaton (Chrysler) were very optimistic that it would work because of the clear strategic advantages. The European market was too small for Daimler, the American market was too small for Chrysler, and there was hardly any overlap between the two companies. Daimler's American activities were limited to the top segment of the market and Chrysler was hardly active at all in Europe. The comments at the announcement of this "merger of equals" were in line with this optimism: "the ideal car marriage" and "the one-hundred percent, ideal combination."

Chrysler and Daimler were two companies with strong and unique heritages. At Chrysler, people were proud of having brought the company from a financial crisis in the early 1990s to success and profitability through intensive cost cutting. At Daimler Benz, people were proud of the products, in particular the quality and technological leadership. Its Mercedes cars were an example of the strengths of German quality and engineering.

Schrempp and Eaton were appointed as joint chairmen and co-CEOs of DaimlerChrysler. The company's legal base would be in Stuttgart, but the company would have dual headquarters in Stuttgart and Auburn Hills.

Initially, the approach to the merger did not really address the cultural differences. Cultural differences were downplayed, under the assumption that there would be no special problems. The initiatives providing cross-cultural information and preparation were limited to "cultural awareness classes" addressing superficial aspects, such as the more formal dress codes in Germany versus the more casual dress code in America, and the more formal German meeting protocol. The leaders concentrated on the operational aspects of the merger. The official strategy was, in order to minimize the risk of a clash of cultures, to allow both groups to maintain their existing cultures. The motto was: one company, one vision, two chairmen, two cultures.

Seemingly, there were no concerns about the big differences between Daimler and Chrysler's corporate cultures, although concerns that a cultural clash could be a major hindrance in realizing the synergies identified before the merger were expressed in the business press. Problems started to emerge as soon as Daimler and Chrysler people started to work together in post-merger integration teams. When we look at some of the differences that came up over time, we recognize most of the nine corporate culture dimensions.

Consistency versus pragmatism. Difference in working styles resulted in the perception on the Chrysler side that rigid Daimler working practices were imposed on their more relaxed style. Daimler people were used to reading lots of documents prior to a meeting, to extensive discussions, and extensive meeting proceedings. Chrysler people were used to less paperwork and short meetings. Chrysler managers were also frustrated by the attention Daimler-Benz managers gave to minor details, such as the design of letterheads.

Individualism versus group orientation. Differences in rewarding practices became a major hindrance. Chrysler managers had higher salaries and bonuses based on individual performance and often earned two or three times as much as their counterparts at Daimler. This huge pay gap between executives and employees was unacceptable by German standards. This was a hindrance when transferring American managers to Germany, where they might earn double the salary of their German bosses. Moreover, senior Chrysler managers had become rich because they could suddenly cash their share options. Daimler also had to get used to differences in loyalty; many talented Chrysler designers left the company soon after the merger.

People centrality versus result centrality. Differences on this dimension became clear when Chrysler decided to cut inventory in North America by shutting down several factories for a week. On the Daimler side, shutting down a factory for a week was not considered to be a normal procedure.

Rational versus inspirational. Daimler's engineering culture was seen as too rational by their American colleagues, who saw themselves as more instinctive, risk taking, and spontaneous.

Egalitarian versus hierarchical. Different ways of decision making and different management styles showed up. Daimler-Benz was known for being formal, bureaucratic, with centralized decision making, and a respect for authority. Chrysler's corporate culture was more egalitarian, characterized by consensus-style management and empowerment of staff. Chrysler allowed mid-level employees to take their own initiatives without having to wait for higher-level approval. At Daimler a decision would go through the bureaucracy: experts would be involved and asked for recommendations. Then it would go for final approval at the top (Vlasic and Stertz, 2000). As a consequence of these differences, Daimler considered that Chrysler's leadership was weak. There were differences in expectations about respect for status, as well. Daimler executives often traveled first class and stayed in top hotels over weekends. Daimler managers were used to keeping office doors closed. Americans interpreted this as secretive behavior, leading to distrust.

Stable continuity versus dynamic change showed up in different ways of planning. Chrysler's corporate culture was focused on taking quick action when a new opportunity was identified, without bothering too much about the details or about the possibility of making mistakes. Germans are trained to think more deductively and the Daimler people were used to making detailed plans and implementing these exactly. Daimler was proud of their methodical approach, while Chrysler encouraged creativity, continuously coming up with new ideas and setting new, "stretched" targets.

Short-term versus long-term orientation. This showed up in communication processes. Chrysler was used to short feedback and correction loops in an almost continuous process of communication about the status of projects and adaptations to changed circumstances. Daimler people expected management to communicate a long-term vision, including clear directives.

During the post-merger process some minor intercultural adjustments in ways of working were made: let the Americans make more detailed plans, and let the Germans take more risks. However, there were no attempts to reconcile the two corporate cultures.

Most of the intercultural issues surfaced soon after the pre-merger phase and could probably have still been resolved if they had received attention from top managers. However, the focus remained on the "hard" business issues, pushing integration in functions such as supplies, sales, and research. In terms of the different possible strategies depicted in Figure 7.2, DaimlerChrysler started with a

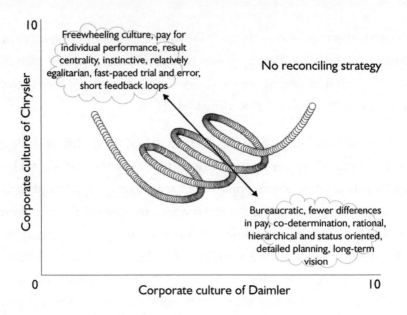

Figure 7.3 Cultural differences between Daimler and Chrysler

compromise strategy, keeping the two cultures separated. However, over time it became clear that, below the surface, Daimler was pursuing a dominating strategy and that Chrysler had no option other than to go for a defensive strategy in reaction. It became clear that Schrempp was the dominant leader who adopted a more and more confrontational style, leading to the departure of top managers from the Chrysler side. Thomas Stallkamp, former president of Chrysler (who had stressed the importance of integrating the two companies) left in September 1999, his successor Jim Holden was forced to leave in November 2000, and co-CEO Bob Eaton had retired in March 2000, leaving Schrempp entirely in charge.

The attitude to intercultural cooperation was now officially "one company, one vision, one chairman, two cultures" (Economist, 2000), but it became more and more clear that Daimler had taken over Chrysler. Later, Schrempp acknowledged that Daimler did not really intend a merger between equals, but that for psychological reasons it could not announce that Chrysler would become a division of Daimler.

Chrysler's president Holden was replaced by Dieter Zetsche, a Daimler executive. Other German executives joined Chrysler in senior positions. Resentment on the Chrysler side increased, because this was seen as imposing Daimler's culture on Chrysler, confirming that it had not been a merger of equals but a sell-out to Daimler. Chrysler now looked more like an operating division of DaimlerChrysler, instead of being a partner in a merger of equals. Many of Chrysler's workers were demoralized by the situation, especially when it was announced that people would be fired. This had a negative effect on cooperation, increased distrust, and has contributed to the fact that the merger has not reached its goals in terms of cost-saving targets, share price, market share, etc.

In September 2003, *Business Week* published a cover story about DaimlerChrysler with the title "Was the Merger a Mistake?" suggesting that Chrysler's huge losses were so threatening for the company that a breakup of the merger was possible.

It is too simple to conclude that the two companies underestimated the cross-border issues in the DaimlerChrysler case. More important than cultural difference itself was that both companies saw their corporate culture as superior, and were not willing to reconcile because they were afraid of dominance by the other party. Postponing addressing the cultural issues led to them fighting it out until the integration process started seriously, with failure to reach merger goals as a result.

DaimlerChrysler versus Renault–Nissan

Now compare this to another strategic cooperation in the car industry with two very different cultures involved: the Renault–Nissan alliance. When Renault's Carlos Ghosn was sent to Nissan to become its CEO he immediately started to address the cultural issues. Ghosn showed that he was aware of the differences and was clear about what needed to be changed at Nissan: getting rid of the seniority system and unprofitable supplier relationships, and introducing accountability, performance pay, a sense of urgency, and a focus on customers. He also showed respect for the need to protect Japanese identity and self-esteem at Nissan and made use of the similarities between French and Japanese corporate cultures: the acceptance of strong leadership, people orientation, and long-term views. In the process, he reconciled the main tensions of organizational integration:

- Radical change from outside and building inside trust through mobilizing Nissan's own managers to identify possibilities for change.
- Creating synergy and respecting cultural identity.

Of course, some culture clashes occurred, such as between Nissan's consensus corporate culture and Renault's more authoritarian style of decision making. And Ghosn was helped by the fact that Nissan badly needed outside pressure and help in order to change and survive. However, we may witness here the emergence of a new type of multicultural leader: Ghosn's multicultural background as a Lebanese by descent, a Brazilian by birth, a Frenchman by citizenship, with a partly American education, seems to make him intuitively sensitive to cultural issues, allowing him to develop a corporate culture at Nissan that combines the best of Japanese and western cultures.

Fortis: how flexible solutions resulted in a solid Dutch–Belgian partnership

Fortis came into being as the result of a merger between Dutch insurance/banking group AMEV/VSB and Belgian insurance company AG in 1990. This merger served as a platform for further growth. Several major acquisitions followed: the Belgian bank ASLK in 1993, the Dutch bank Mees Pierson (private banking and investment banking) in 1996, the Belgian Generale bank in 1998, and in 2000 the Dutch insurance company ASR, making Fortis a leading European financial service provider. Fortis is one of the few examples of a real cross-border merger. Although acquisitions changed the balance in invested capital, at least temporarily, Fortis managed to maintain a 50–50 equality formula between its Dutch and Belgian activities (Prud'homme and Schrijen, 2002). Prior to Fortis, there was a history of failed Dutch–Belgian merger attempts. Although the Netherlands and Belgium are neighboring countries, the cultural differences are great. The question is, therefore, which particular factors made this one succeed? There was a key role for the two people who acted as joint chairmen from 1990–2000: Hans Bartelds (the Dutch former chairman of AMEV/VSB), who was described as a man of equality, harmony, and compromise, with a down-to-earth and low-key style, and Maurice Lippens (the Belgian former Chairman of AG) who was described as charismatic, a networker, and a relationship builder who brought people together. Their cooperation symbolized the merger: almost opposite personalities, but with complementary skills.

To understand why it worked we need to look at the merger process before we look at the differences between the corporate cultures:

- The attitude of both leaders towards dealing with cultural differences was that they saw the effects of different cultures as enriching, and that they tried to understand, manage, and exploit the variety, instead of ignoring the differences or trying to impose one way and kill the diversity. The focus was on making everybody aware that the different corporate cultures both worked by looking first at what they could do together, in a very market-oriented approach.

- The long pre-merger phase (eight months from the start of the talks to the announcement of the deal) was used to find out how things worked on the other side, taking the time to get to know each other, to build respect and trust, and to agree on turning the deal into a win–win situation. This investment in understanding each other turned out to be extremely important.

- The equality principle was reflected in maintaining parity between Dutch and Belgian members in the executive committee and in the dual leadership. The agreement to do the merger on the basis of equality meant that both parties were willing to share power. Parity was maintained to give the feeling on both sides that there would be a power balance between the Dutch and the Belgians, thus avoiding the risk of a dominating–defensive strategy.

Differences in working methods between the Netherlands and Belgium were encountered right from the start of the merger talks. The merger process that led to the present Fortis organization was full of dilemmas. The way Fortis's leadership handled the process was crucial in successfully reconciling these dilemmas. We will use the nine dimensions of corporate culture to analyse the key ones.

Consistency versus pragmatism. A frequent problem in Dutch–Belgian business cooperation is that the Dutch are seen as coming in with standardized solutions: theirs. The dilemma that Fortis faced in the merger process was this: Do we capture everything in formal agreements and documents or do we let the process evolve? Fortis' leaders reconciled this dilemma by bringing in lawyers at the start of the process to draw up all the agreements and documents, and doing this so thoroughly that they never had to look at the official documents again. One of the main differences between Dutch and Belgian corporate culture is the governance structure. The Netherlands works on the basis of a two-tier board structure: the Board of Non-Executive Directors and the Board of Directors. Belgium has a one-tier Board of Directors, which includes the Executive Directors and the Non-Executive Directors. Fortis decided not to integrate the two governance structures right from the start. The leaders let the process evolve by installing a dual holding structure and postponing a final decision on how to integrate the governance. That was possible because there was trust: "When there is no trust, you want to have everything resolved beforehand" (Hans Bartelds, quoted in Prud'homme and Schrijen, 2002). Both parties, however, agreed on the principle of equality and sharing power. Through agreeing on sharing power, trust was established and Fortis could let the process of integrating corporate governance evolve. Although the equality principle was challenged several times, this approach saw Fortis through to a successful merger.

Individualism versus group orientation and *people centrality versus result centrality*. In the Netherlands, it is perfectly acceptable to come to a meeting with five people, discuss the problem in depth while there, and to have everyone give an opinion, sometimes opposite to that of the chairperson. In Belgium, this would be seen as loss of face for the person in the chair. The preferred way of doing the equivalent would be to have informal meetings with each of these five people separately, discuss the pros and cons of different possible solutions, and have the work done by the time the formal meeting starts.

People centrality in Belgian business culture leads to a high importance for personal networks, which means that influential people need to be involved in decisions even when involvement in the decision is not strictly part of their task. This has an impact for decision making processes as well, because it is not always possible to make agreements during a meeting with only the people around the table. Fortis found out that through respecting differences in decision making processes, commitment to decisions actually increases.

Rational versus inspirational. The dual leadership of the more rational Bartelds and the charismatic Lippens has been an important factor in reconciling this dilemma.

Egalitarian versus hierarchical leadership. There were clear differences between the corporate cultures in terms of dealing with hierarchy and authority. In the Netherlands an executive committee works like a flat organization in which the chair is nothing more than a *primus inter pares*. In Belgium the Chief Executive Officer is clearly the one who takes the final decision and the others have their own areas of responsibility. Fortis reconciled these differences by combining decisiveness and consensus.

Internal drive versus responsiveness. Any merger across borders faces a dilemma between decentralizing to retain local identities and local responsiveness versus centralizing and shaping a global identity. Fortis has reconciled this dilemma by letting local identities exist for a limited period of time, while working on creating a global identity, and without becoming a centralized organization. In Fortis, only a few key areas are controlled from the center, such as external communications and risk management.

Differences in time orientation. The differences between the Dutch more long-term, strategic planning orientation and the more flexible approach in the Belgian corporate culture were reconciled by having clear, long-term strategic objectives – not in order to predict the future, but to make Fortis alert to any possibilities for change offered by the environment.

This 1990 merger was the start of a process that has never stopped. The Fortis culture is still evolving. An important step has been the nomination of one CEO in 2000 and abandoning the concept of parity between Dutch and Belgians at all levels. Anton van Rossum, Fortis' new CEO, is a Dutch national but he knows Belgium well, as he has lived and worked there since 1982. He speaks Dutch, French, and English and has shown his ability to build bridges across both company and national cultures.

The Fortis case shows that integrating corporate cultures requires the willingness and ability to create integrated diversity. The colorful Fortis logo, introduced in 1999, symbolizes this. The motto associated with the logo, "solid partners, flexible solutions" is perhaps one of the best examples of what the power of merging corporate cultures should be. Fortis manages to be consistent by being diverse, flexible, and decentralized. Instead of imposing a centralized bureaucracy, Fortis builds a global identity by creating a "we" feeling, being clear about some shared principles, creating centers of excellence, empowering people to share best practices, and agreeing on one direction, the growth strategy: "You don't have to be the same, as long as you share the same goals and objectives."

A European–Korean merger

The next case in this chapter is a merger between the divisions of a European company and a Korean company – we will call them Eurco and Koreaco. At the announcement of this merger, Eurco and Koreaco (until then competitors in the field) were described as the ideal synergetic partners with respect to products, markets served, manufacturing capabilities, and technological leadership. The joint venture was a 50–50 merger with a mixed European/Korean management team. Table 7.1 gives an analysis of the differences on the nine dimensions of corporate culture.

All the differences in Table 7.1 were experienced in practice. Figure 7.4 gives an example of how the differences in expectations of leadership were reconciled.

Companies involved in merger, acquisitions and alliance processes should realize that the value of their own company and of their prospective partner lies mostly in the culture, not in the buildings and other "hard" assets. At THT we are frequently approached a few months – or even years – after a merger or acquisition to help resolve conflicts related to corporate culture differences, just because the

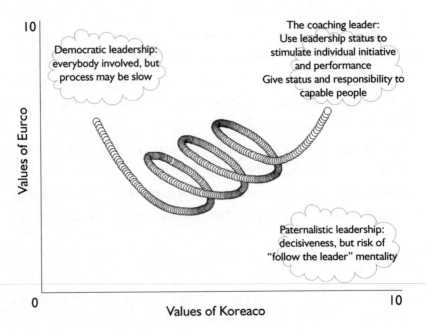

Figure 7.4 Merger between Eurco and Koreaco – reconciling differences in expectations of leadership

Table 7.1 Cultural differences in a European–Korean merger

Corporate culture values – Eurco	Corporate culture values – Koreaco	Corporate culture dimension
Global standards, formal systems, procedures, rules, responsibilities, extensive documentation. A deal is a deal.	Pragmatic solutions for unique situations. Importance of informal organization. Rules and systems are often ambiguous. Ask more concessions after a deal.	Consistency versus pragmatism
Individual initiative and accountability. Expressing individual opinions. Individuals allowed to make mistakes. Respect for private life expected. Direct communication, direct criticism, direct "no" is acceptable.	Group loyalty and support. Sharing information only with (Korean) in-group. Making a mistake is less acceptable. Importance of activities to build community; prepared to sacrifice private time for the company. Indirect communication to avoid loss of face; use of intermediaries to communicate difficult messages.	Individualism versus group orientation
Proud of success in the past: why should we partner with a less sophisticated company?	Cooperation with a former competitor does not mean that we stop competing with them.	Partnership versus competing
Focus on task relationship Importance of quality of life.	Importance of personal relationships. Strong work discipline.	People centrality versus result centrality
Rational, unemotional styles prevail.	Visibility of top management. Charismatic leadership, emotional and sometimes confrontational styles prevail.	Rational versus inspirational

Corporate culture values – Eurco	Corporate culture values – Koreaco	Corporate culture dimension
Leader first among equals. Meetings are for exchanging opinions, building consensus. Everybody involved in decision making. Openly challenging or contradicting authority is acceptable. Showing respect for status not expected.	Leaders have power and status to take decisions and change decisions. Meetings are for communicating/ affirming decisions. Challenging authority not acceptable. Status is a function of gender, seniority, education, hierarchical position, connections. Status expressed by symbols. Showing respect for status expected.	Egalitarian versus hierarchical
Technology and product push	"Customer is king": high expectations of responsiveness, flexibility, hospitality.	Internal drive versus responsiveness
Detailed planning. Prefer step-by-step approach.	Aggressive growth and "go for it" culture: life moves at a hectic pace, it is impossible to anticipate all circumstances. May drop planned activity when other priority comes up.	Stable continuity versus dynamic change
Carefully considering consequences of future plans. Focus too much on long-term plan, not on action.	Focus on the here and now, speedy implementation of small improvements: action now.	Short-term versus long-term orientation

cultural issues were ignored in the focus on "hard" issues at the time of the deal. On the basis of these experiences, we have drawn up the following list of common mistakes in mergers and acquisitions:

- Ignoring the cultural issues.
- Only paying attention to the "superficial" cultural issues; for example, intercultural communication.
- Using the term "merger" for what is in reality an acquisition.
- "Integration" interpreted as "adaptation to the dominant partner."
- Using the rhetoric of "marriages made in heaven," "perfect fit," and "synergy" to hide the real motives for the merger or acquisition in order to protect personal or business interests.
- Underestimating the competence of the partner.

CHAPTER 8

Deriving strength from the tension between seemingly opposite values

n this final chapter we argue that it is a prerequisite for successful organizations to reconcile the variety of organizational cultures of which they consist in order to face the challenging world in which they operate. All companies face dilemmas in the current business environment, seemingly conflicting values leading to major tensions. The solution is not to choose one of the extremes. The solution is to derive strength from the tension between seemingly opposite values in a continuous process of reconciliation. Most of the successful organizations that we have discussed reconcile the major tensions that are facing them.

THE NINE MAJOR DILEMMAS

The last five years of research at THT have given us the opportunity to look at the dilemmas that were raised by our clients. We have asked all participants in our workshops to use WebCue, our web-based assessment system. As preparation they were asked to reveal the issues, the challenges, the problems they were facing in business. They were asked to phrase their challenge as "on the one hand…versus on the other hand…" In other words, we tried to make the participants see their problem and issues as a dilemma. Upon analysis we found dilemmas related to all the nine dimensions of corporate culture discussed in this book. These are the nine major dilemmas that we have identified, including the corporate culture labels we've attached to them:

1. Having global standards while being locally responsive (consistency versus pragmatism).

2. Emphasizing individual initiative and performance while making people cooperate in teams, across business units, and other organizational boundaries (individualism versus group orientation).

3. Keeping a competitive edge while building deep partnerships with suppliers, competitors, and customers (competing versus partnerships).

4. Accomplishing results while building an environment in which people can thrive and develop themselves (result centrality versus people centrality).

5. Working towards rational goals while inspiring people with a higher level purpose, principles, and values (rational versus inspirational).

6. Showing decisiveness while being democratic (hierarchical versus egalitarian).

7. Having a strong internal drive while being open to developments in the outside world (internal drive versus responsiveness).

8. Ensuring stability and continuity while investing in innovation and change (stable continuity versus dynamic change).

9. Delivering short-term shareholder value while thinking long term (short-term versus long-term orientation).

Business developments of the past decade, such as the increasing focus on shareholder value, have meant that companies are inclined to develop corporate cultures which try to solve these dilemmas by going for a set of dominant corporate values at an extreme end of the value dilemma. However, corporate cultures that lose their sense of balance for a longer period of time inevitably lose their strengths and turn these into weaknesses. For example, the impact of focus on short-term shareholder value goes further than the disappearance of lifetime employment and job security, and the increasing impact of work obligations on private life. Examples in this book have shown that it can easily promote survival behavior, resulting in corporate cultures characterized by fear, denial, self-interest, and distrust, and in loss of employee loyalty and – in the end – customer loyalty as well.

STRENGTHS AND WEAKNESS OF CORPORATE CULTURES

Short-term orientation is just one of the corporate culture value orientations that turns into a negative when taken to the extreme. Each extreme corporate culture value orientation has its strengths and weaknesses.

Focus on standards for the benefit of the efficiency of the organization (consistency) can lead to a culture dictated by systems and job descriptions. Scientific management once reigned supreme in organization theory, but it committed suicide because of extremism. The "homo efficientis" looks very much at the means and is not always goal directed. However, taking the need for local flexibility (pragmatism) to its extreme will lead to chaos.

Dividing organizations into ever smaller parts in order to define individual responsibilities and accountabilities, and linking these to individual performance incentives, leads to compartmentalization and a lack of collaboration (individualism). However, taking group orientation to its extreme makes individuals hide behind the group.

Taking competing to the extreme can lead to self-defeat. Taking partnership orientation to the extreme can lead to "cuddling each other into bankruptcy."

Result centrality leads to judging employees only on their contribution for corporate profit, but an organization is more than a collection of robots that need to operate in the way of the "homo economicus." However, the opposite model – the "homo socialis" –

can destroy itself as well, when people centrality and thriving on personal relationships are taken to the extreme.

Rational cultures are at their best realistic and analytical, but tend to have problems in seeing the whole picture. Inspirational cultures are at their best driven by passion, but this often goes together with a tendency to take unrealistic decisions.

Hierarchical cultures may kill themselves because of exaggerated power politics and succession problems. Egalitarian culture, taken to the extreme, may result in lost democratic leadership.

Internal drive taken to the extreme leads to pushing technology that nobody needs. Responsiveness leads in its extreme to a different product for every single customer.

Focus on stability and continuity can lead to a sluggish culture, too slow for adaptation to the ever increasing speeds of the societies in which it operates. Dynamic change is, at its best, a culture where people thrive on learning. The downside of this dominant culture is that when it grows it becomes too differentiated and chaotic. The "homo apprendis" has its limitations in growing environments.

Short-term focus, as discussed, is supposed to lead to cultures where members are financially motivated for the benefit of shareholders in a very effective way. However this purely financial and instrumental view can also lead to anonymous money-shufflers thinking that one can become rich without adding any value. The intention to serve the long-term interest of all stakeholders may well end up serving nobody's interests if lack of short-term profitability leads to bankruptcy.

The dominant mindset prescribed by the management literature switches back and forth between extremes, that is from "homo economicus" to "homo socialis," and from "homo efficientis" to "homo apprendis." Perhaps the time has come for an organizational mindset where people integrate opposites: the "homo reconciliens." This is the person who works in organizations where opposites and dilemmas are being reconciled at higher levels.

In line with the criteria of good individual leadership, we need to fundamentally redefine and reequilibrate the criteria for the quality of the collective organization. Many traditional methods for determining leadership qualities base their score on a number of criteria, where the extremes of the scales are mutually exclusive. Take the ISTJ (introvert, sensitive, thinking, and judging) score, for example, the most popular type for a successful manager using the Myers–Briggs typology: all of those qualities exclude their mirror images. In order to ascertain the essential qualities of a leader we need to judge how well this person integrates opposites in tension. Effective leaders will use emotions to increase their power of thinking, use analysis in order to test the larger whole, and use imagination in order to make realistic decisions (Trompenaars and Hampden-Turner, 2003). The same applies to the organizations in which these leaders operate.

THE NINE GOLDEN DILEMMAS AND THE RECONCILIATION SCOREBOARD

At THT we have done research on the nine major tensions and dilemmas discussed above with ten blue chip organizations. The research focused on whether we could map the value of an organization in an alternative way by the degree to which these organizations integrated tensions. We hoped that the average score would give us a much better insight than pure financial and technical analyses. Some examples speak for themselves. In this way the reconciliation of the dilemma between efficiency of the internal organization and the development of the employees are of prime importance for the value of an organization. Here the "homo efficientis" meets the "homo socialis." On the field of tension between financial short-term results and investments in people for the long term, the "homo economicus" meets the "homo apprendis." The development of technology needs to reconcile itself with the demand of the market in such a way that the market helps decide which technologies to push. On the other hand, the push of technology will need to help determine which markets one wants to be pulled by. The need for consistencies in the global organization needs to be fine-tuned with the need for local flexibility and sensitivity.

Until now, only managers have scored our nine "reconciliation scoreboards." Very soon we will ask clients, suppliers, and financial analysts to provide their opinions and score their organizations on the nine "golden dilemmas" according to the methodology and format described below. On each of the nine scorecards we will ask the relevant group to indicate the importance of the dilemma at stake on a scale of 1 to 10 so we can weigh the relevance differently for different organizations.

This might lead to an alternative new way of evaluating how value is created in organizations: by continuously managing the tension between seemingly opposing objectives, which are both necessary to deliver short-term and long-term value for all stakeholders.

Let's look in detail at the nine "golden dilemmas." There are scorecards provided for each one.

1. Global consistency versus local flexibility and decentral customization (pragmatism)

One of the most frequently discussed tensions is this: on the one hand there is the need for (global) consistency and (central) standards and on the other hand the need for (local) flexibility and (decentral) customization in order to serve the client better. The question here is whether the systems, processes, and leadership in the central organization serve the decentralized operations optimally. Conversely, the challenge is whether the local best practices are being taken seriously so that they serve the larger organization best. The dilemma is illustrated in Figure 8.1.

Scorecard 1 is evaluated as follows:

All organizations face a challenge of how to align the internal organization in order for it to be more effective to its external environment. One argument normally dominates:

    (A) The need for (central) standards to increase (global) consistency

    (B) The need for (local) flexibility and (decentral) customization to serve the client better.

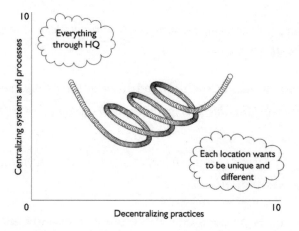

Figure 8.1 The central organization versus local practices dilemma

1.   Which of these priorities is more fulfilling to you personally?

2.   Judged by how it is measured and what it promotes, which is more
        important to the organization?

Suppose you could allocate 0–10 points to Priority A, the need for (global)
consistency and (central) standards and 0–10 points to Priority B, the need
for (local) flexibility and (decentral) customization to serve the client better,
where would you locate your organization? (Place an X). Where would you
like to see it move? (Place an O there).

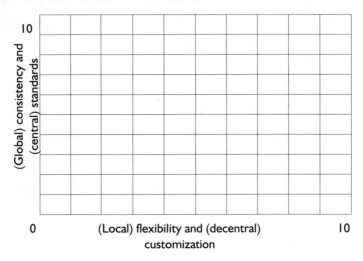

3.   What organizational measures can the firm implement to move closer
        to the 10/10 position?

4.   On a scale from 1 (irrelevant) to 10 (crucial) how would you score the
        relevance of this dilemma for the (future) success of the organization?

2. Team orientation (group orientation) versus individual creativity (individualism)

This dilemma is perhaps one of the more frequently encountered
ones. Within a group-oriented culture one likes to develop loyal

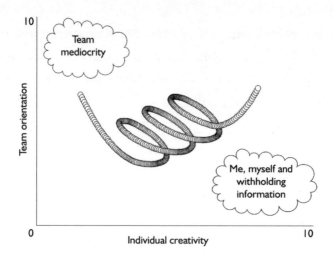

Figure 8.2 Team orientation versus individual creativity

teams. On the other hand, just as often the organization is in need of creative solutions where individuals take risks and stand out. In the analysis of the dilemmas that our clients revealed we have seen that it is felt that team orientation is often sacrificed for the creative individuals. Therefore the second major dilemma is the famous tension between team orientation and individual creativity, shown in Figure 8.2.

Scorecard 2 is evaluated as follows:

Organizations are facing a tension between orientations toward teams and the creativity of individuals. There are different opinions about what leads to the success of an organization:

(A) *An organization can best go for commitment to teams*

(B) *An organization can best go for individual creativity*

1. *Which of these priorities is more fulfilling to you personally?*

2. *Judged by how it is measured and what it promotes, which is more important to your organization?*

Suppose you could allocate 0–10 points to Priority A, team orientation and 0–10 points to Priority B, individual creativity, Where would you locate your organization? (Place an X there). Where would you like to see it move? (Place an O at that point).

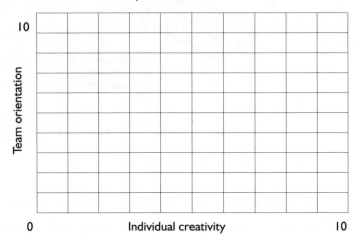

3. What organizational measures can the firm implement to move closer to the 10/10 position?

4. On a scale from 1 (irrelevant) to 10 (crucial) how would you score the relevance of this dilemma for the (future) success of the organization?

3. Competing versus cooperating (partnership orientation)

This is a dilemma that has only recently started to come up in the WebCue dilemmas. It was raised as follows: On the one hand, our management expects us to compete aggressively to survive cut-throat competition in fast changing markets, for instance by breakthrough innovations. On the other hand our management forms joint ventures and alliances with our competitors and expects us to start sharing R&D with them, releasing information about unique innovations which we should keep to ourselves. The dilemma looks like Figure 8.3.

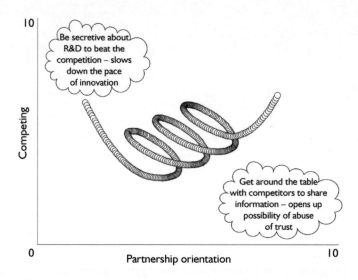

Figure 8.3   Competing versus partnership orientation

Scorecard 3 is evaluated as follows:

Organizations are facing a tension between competing fiercely in their markets and forging partnerships with competitors to set standards and reduce costs in R&D. There are different opinions on what leads to the success of an organization:

> *(A) An organization can best go for competing aggressively.*

> *(B) An organization can best go for forging partnerships.*

1.   Which of these priorities is more fulfilling to you personally?

2.   Judged by how it is measured and what it promotes, which is more important to your organization?

Suppose you could allocate 0–10 points to Priority A, competing, and 0–10 points to Priority B, partnership orientation, where would you locate your organization? (Place an X). Where would you like to see it move? (Place an O).

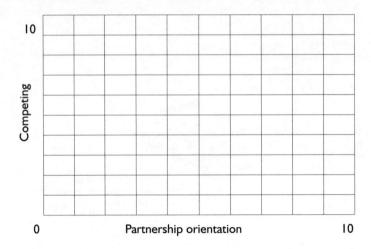

3.   *What organizational measures can the firm implement to move closer to the 10/10 position?*

4.   *On a scale from 1 (irrelevant) to 10 (crucial) how would you score the relevance of this dilemma for the (future) success of the organization?*

4. Efficiency of business processes (result centrality) versus developing human resources (people centrality)

This is quite a classical dilemma, one well described by the tension within socio-technical systems. The main dilemma the organization is facing is how to align the efficiency of business processes with the motivation of the human parts of the system. Versions of this that were raised in our WebCue dilemmas were task orientation versus people orientation and organizational predictability versus staff empowerment. The dilemma can best be shown as in Figure 8.4.

Scorecard 4 is evaluated as follows:

A main dilemma the organization is facing is that of how to align the efficiency of business processes with the motivation of the human parts of the system. There are two extreme orientations according to which an organization can be successful:

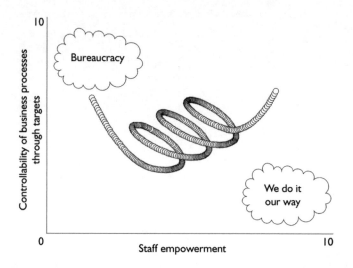

Figure 8.4 Efficiency versus staff empowerment dilemma

(A) *We can best orient ourselves on getting the basic organizational tasks accomplished and as such achieve organizational predictability.*

(B) *We can best orient ourselves on giving freedom to our human resources by empowering our staff.*

1. *Which of these priorities is more fulfilling to you personally?*

2. *Judged by how it is measured and what it promotes, which is more important to your organization?*

Suppose you could allocate 0–10 points to Priority A, predictability of organizational tasks and 0–10 points to Priority B, empowerment of staff. Where would you locate your organization? (Place an X). Where would you like to see it move? (Place an O).

3. *What organizational measures can the firm implement to move closer to the 10/10 position?*

4. *On a scale from 1 (irrelevant) to 10 (crucial) how would you score the relevance of this dilemma for the (future) success of the organization?*

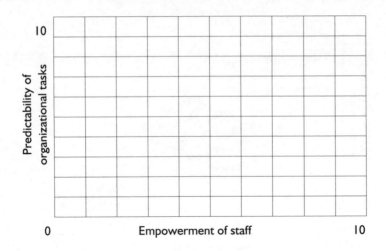

0   Empowerment of staff   10

5. Grand visions (inspirational) versus keeping the business going (rational)

This is another tension that recently started to appear more and more in our WebCue. It was raised, for instance, as "on the one hand our management has grand visions of having a reputation of being the frontrunner in the corporate responsibility movement, but on the other hand they want us to keep business volume and profit up so that we are forced to take risks which may damage our reputation on the environmental and social dimension." The dilemma looks like the one in Figure 8.5.

Scorecard 5 is evaluated as follows:

A main dilemma the organization is facing is one of how to align inspiring ideals with rational targets. There are two extreme orientations according to which an organization can be successful:

    (A) We need inspiring ideals to lead us into the future.

    (B) We can best focus on rational goals.

1.   *Which of these priorities is more fulfilling to you personally?*

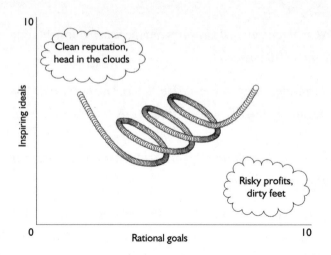

Figure 8.5 Inspirational vision versus rational goals dilemma

2. *Judged by how it is measured and what it promotes, which is more important to your organization?*

Suppose you could allocate 0–10 points to Priority A, inspiring ideals and 0–10 points to Priority B, rational targets. Where would you locate your organization? (Place an X). Where would you like to see it move? (Place an O).

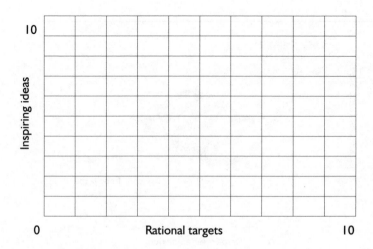

3.   *What organizational measures can the firm implement to move closer to the 10/10 position?*

4.   *On a scale from 1 (irrelevant) to 10 (crucial) how would you score the relevance of this dilemma for the (future) success of the organization?*

6. Participating employees (egalitarian) versus respect for authority (hierarchical)

This tension has not been raised often in our database of dilemmas at THT. That does not mean that it is not an issue. The sixth dilemma concerns the relationship between both mentioned parties. If too much decision-making power is given to the employees the company becomes a lost democratic leadership, with too little left for management to direct. Conversely, once management gets too much say, employees are often constrained and feel too dependent on the latest mood of their managers, such as the need to follow their direction. Obviously reconciliation lies in a form of codetermination. This is illustrated in Figure 8.6.

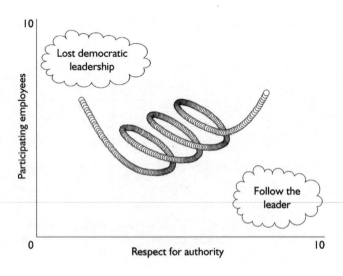

Figure 8.6   Participating employees versus respect for authority

Scorecard 6 is evaluated as follows:

There are differing views on how to make an organization most effective.

(A) *The first view is that for the most effective organization one needs to have employees participate in decision making.*

(B) *The alternative view is that, first and foremost, there should be respect for authority in the organization.*

1.   *Which of these approaches do you personally prefer?*

2.   *Which approach prevails at your organization in: (a) Asia, (b) Europe, (c) the Americas?*

Suppose you could allocate 0–10 points to Viewpoint A, participating employees, and 0–10 points to Viewpoint B, respect for authority. Where on the grid would you locate your organization? (Place an X). Where would you like to see it move? (Place an O).

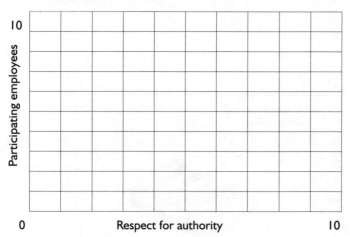

3.   *What organizational measures can the firm implement to move closer to the 10/10 position?*

4.   *On a scale from 1 (irrelevant) to 10 (crucial) how would you score the relevance of this dilemma for the (future) success of the organization?*

7. New client development (responsiveness) versus push of technology (internal drive)

This tension develops when a company has enjoyed great operational success, often based on technology or service leadership but, with the maturing of its markets, customers have gained more power and are demanding customized products/services and higher levels of personal service. The tension relates to the challenges employees are facing to "pull" what the company produces toward the emerging needs of the market. The major issue at stake is to connect the internal drive culture, leading to the talent of technology push with the responsiveness-oriented world of market pull in order to achieve a culture of inventiveness. The success of an organization is dependent on the integration of both areas. The push of technology needs to help you in deciding what markets you want to be pulled by. And the pull of the market needs to help you in knowing what technologies to push. The dilemma is illustrated in Figure 8.7.

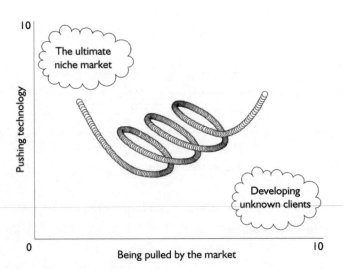

Figure 8.7 The technology push versus responsiveness to customers dilemma

Scorecard 7 is evaluated as follows:

An organization can get its strength through orienting itself in two diverse ways:

(A) *Externally – develop markets and channels by being pulled by markets and opportunities out there.*

(B) *Internally – develop technologies and products or by pushing technologies and products even further.*

1. *Which of these priorities is more fulfilling to you personally?*

2. *Judged by how it is measured and what it promotes, which is more important to your organization?*

Suppose you could allocate 0–10 points to Priority A, market pull and 0–10 points to Priority B, technology push, where would you locate your organization? (Place an X). Where would you like to see it move? (Place an O).

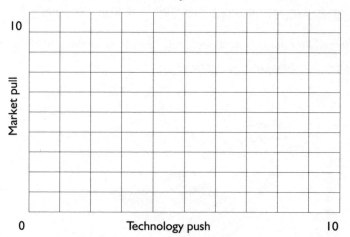

3. *What organizational measures can the firm implement to move closer to the 10/10 position?*

4. *On a scale from 1 (irrelevant) to 10 (crucial) how would you score the relevance of this dilemma for the (future) success of the organization?*

8. Planning orientation (stable continuity) versus freedom to develop and learn by errors (dynamic change)

Very frequently employees feel a pressure to work according to plans that are carefully set by management, even though they feel that learning from mistakes and experiments, followed by redefining plans, would be a better way to ensure continuity. Graphically this tension could be best presented as in Figure 8.8.

Scorecard 8 is evaluated as follows:

In motivating employees there are two extreme methods to consider

(A) *We can best motivate employees by making them work according to carefully prepared plans.*

(B) *We can best motivate employees by allowing them to make errors from which they can learn.*

1. *Which of these priorities is more fulfilling to you personally?*

2. *Judged by how it is measured and what it promotes, which is more important to your organization?*

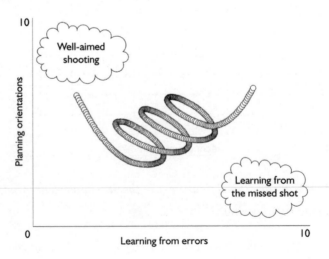

Figure 8.8 Planning orientation versus learning from experimental errors

Suppose you could allocate 0–10 points to Priority A, planning orientation and 0–10 points to Priority B, freedom to develop and learn by errors, where would you locate your organization? (Place an X). Where would you like to see it move? (Place an O).

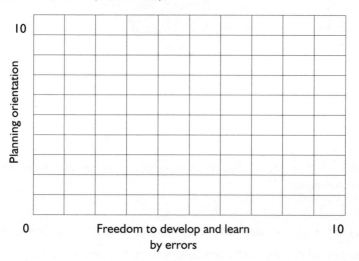

3. *What organizational measures can the firm implement to move closer to the 10/10 position?*

4. *On a scale from 1 (irrelevant) to 10 (crucial) how would you score the relevance of this dilemma for the (future) success of the organization?*

9. Long-term value for all stakeholders (long-term orientation) versus shareholder value (short-term orientation)

This important dilemma is perhaps one of the most underestimated ones. After the separation of ownership and management many dilemmas were created that summarize the tension between a fair return in the short term and an even better return in the long term. In the analysis of the dilemmas that our clients have revealed, we can see that it is felt that long-term value for all stakeholders (including employees, communities, the environment, suppliers) is too often

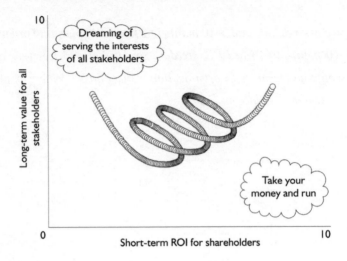

Figure 8.9 The long-term value for all stakeholders versus short-term share-holder value dilemma

sacrificed for the shareholders' quarterly returns. Therefore the ninth major dilemma is the tension between serving the long-term needs of all stakeholders (by investments in the development of people, in supportive communities, in sustainable growth, and in long-term relationships with suppliers and customers) and the often short-term need to pay a reasonable return to shareholders. It is illustrated in Figure 8.9.

Scorecard 9 is evaluated as follows:

There are two important priorities for the success of an organization.

(A) *We best serve our organization by investing in long-term value for all stakeholders: putting responsibility for all stakeholders first.*

(B) *We best serve our organization by focusing on getting the best returns for our shareholders: putting profitability first.*

1. *Which of these priorities is more fulfilling to you personally?*

2. *Judged by how it is measured and what it promotes, which is more important to your organization?*

Suppose you could allocate 0–10 points to Priority A, investing in long term value for all stakeholders, and 0–10 points to Priority B, focusing on short term ROI for shareholders, where would you locate your organization? (Place an X). Where would you like to see it move? (Place an O).

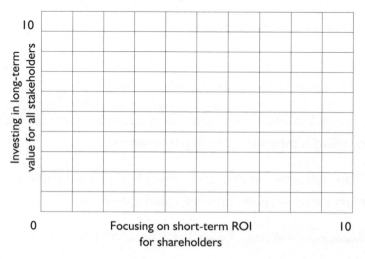

3. *What organizational measures can the firm implement to move closer to the 10/10 position?*

4. *On a scale from 1 (irrelevant) to 10 (crucial) how would you score the relevance of this dilemma for the (future) success of the organization?*

Through–through thinking

By asking respondents to indicate how they view the current (position X) and ideal corporate culture (position O) in the scorecards, we get an indication of in which direction they would like to see the culture move. In order to change the current culture (the current reality), we need to reconcile it with the ideal. The only way of moving towards this ideal is through mobilizing current realities.

Reconciling the nine golden dilemmas of corporate culture is an ongoing process of through–through thinking, as in the following reconciliations:

1. Develop global standards *through* being locally responsive.

2. Stimulate individual initiative and performance *through* making people cooperate in teams, across business units, and other organizational boundaries.

3. Keep a competitive edge *through* building deep partnerships with suppliers, competitors, and customers.

4. Accomplish results *through* building an environment in which people can thrive and develop themselves.

5. Work towards rational goals *through* inspiring people by a higher level purpose, principles, and values.

6. Realize decisiveness *through* being democratic.

7. Develop a strong internal drive *through* being open to developments in the outside world.

8. Stability and continuity *through* investing in innovation and change.

9. Deliver short-term shareholder value *through* investing in long-term value for all stakeholders.

In this chapter we have argued that successful organizations derive their strength from the tension between seemingly opposite values by reconciling the nine fundamental dilemmas of corporate culture. The reconciliation scorecards reveal where a corporate culture is now and where people want to see it move in order to face the challenges of the business environment. The strength of the reconciling corporate culture model is that it offers more than just a tool for mapping and understanding corporate cultures. Through–through thinking offers a dynamic model for changing corporate cultures from "current" to a position closer to the "10,10" position on the scorecard.

Conclusion

Today's business environment is much more complex, interdependent, unpredictable, and unstable than it was just a decade ago. Developing and sustaining the success of an organization requires coping with ongoing change in this complex environment. It is not surprising, therefore, that corporate culture change initiatives are proliferating.

However, what is often not understood is that changing a corporate culture is a contradiction in terms. One of the roles of corporate culture is to provide stability, focus, direction, and guidance, and because of this corporate cultures have the tendency to persist. The paradox of change across corporate cultures is that in order to change corporate cultures, they need to be in flux in the first place. The concept of the reconciling corporate culture that we have introduced in this book offers a dynamic model for creating, understanding, and changing corporate cultures "in flux." Reconciling corporate cultures have an inherent capacity to connect seemingly opposing value orientations in an ongoing dialogue. This way of looking at corporate cultures acknowledges that providing stability goes hand in hand with tension and potential conflict between opposing value orientations. In reconciling corporate cultures, the energy in this tension is used to sustain ongoing change.

One of the reasons that many "traditional" corporate culture change initiatives fail is that they are implicitly based on the old "unfreeze–move–refreeze" approach to change: changing a corporate culture from one fixed set of value polarities to a different set of value polarities and then "refreezing" it. Such cultures may actually prohibit the successful implementation of change initiatives.

Our model allows for looking at change as something that is necessary to preserve continuity and identity, so that change becomes a way of life.

Another reason why many traditional corporate culture change initiatives fail is that they treat the "hard side" of change (e.g. growth, increasing shareholder value, improving performance, reducing costs, improving innovative capability) and the "soft side" (or human side) of change as separate issues, and address these independently or in sequence. For instance, change approaches such as reengineering address the soft side mainly by offering a set of techniques to deal with resistance that might hinder the hard side of the change process.

Our reconciling corporate culture model acknowledges the inherent tension between change focused on hard issues and soft issues, and acknowledges that this tension inherently triggers resistance because corporate cultures are created and changed by human beings who have their own interests and identities to defend. The concept of the reconciling corporate culture combines addressing the hard and soft side in a continuous process. In this approach, resistance is not seen as a hindrance for change, but as a prerequisite for it. Without resistance, no real change is possible.

As a result of the widespread failure of change initiatives, many managers have started to doubt whether changing a corporate culture is possible at all. Indeed, many approaches to change are too narrowly focused to have a chance of success. The ever-increasing speed of change in the business environment requires an approach to changing corporate cultures that does not shy away from contradictions and complexity. Change across corporate cultures is feasible when all nine dilemmas of corporate culture are reconciled in the change process itself, so that seemingly contradictory approaches to change reinforce each other in a unifying model for change.

Change focused on structures and procedures versus change focused on supporting autonomous developments

Change processes do need to address structures and procedures, for example in order to realize economies of scale and operational discipline. However, extreme focus on structures and procedures will lead to centralism and "centocracies." Change processes also need to address supporting and coaching decentralized activities to develop a more entrepreneurial mindset. However, extreme focus on supporting autonomous developments will lead to lack of control. In reconciling corporate cultures, change takes place by learning from decentralized activities which supportive systems and structures will help in further developing an entrepreneurial mindset.

Change focused on developing individuals versus change focused on creating community

Change processes which take a focus on the individual as the driver for value creation to the extreme may end up with all the negatives of a fragmented organization. Change processes which take a focus on building community to the extreme may end up in "team-oriented" cultures in which talents are hidden rather than developed. In a reconciling corporate culture change takes place by leveraging the talents of individuals through incentives that stimulate exchanging knowledge and taking pride in the achievements of others.

Change focused on creating a competing spirit versus change focused on creating a collaborative spirit

Change processes do need to address creating a "winning spirit" but too much focus on competing will have adverse effects on willingness to cooperate in alliances and other partnerships. We witnessed one company organize a mountaineering trip for those employees who had just been assigned to a joint venture with a new business partner, in order to create a spirit of being unbeatable – a trip which turned out to be detrimental for the group's collaborative spirit. However, taking the collaborative spirit to the extreme can lead to undesirable "cozy collusions." In reconciling corporate cultures, change takes place by developing boundary spanning (the ability to work across organizational boundaries) as a core competence.

Change focused on improving business results versus change focused on people issues

Change processes do need to address business results but an extreme focus on targets and results will lead to "change by fear." Many consultancy companies have used the slogan "change is pain" in their change management approaches. Change processes also need to address people issues by paying attention to personal needs and interests; however, an extreme focus on people issues leads to a "caring corporation" in which people, as we've noted, "hug and kiss each other into bankruptcy." Reconciling corporate cultures, through paying attention to the problems and dilemmas that people face in their day today work, discover how change impacts on people and how people can benefit from change. Cost reduction and stretched, ambitious targets can then be achieved through investing in people development, e.g., training.

Motivate for change by focusing on hard data and measurements versus motivate for change by an inspiring philosophy or vision

Change initiatives focused on data and measurements run the risk of ending up in a "toolkit approach." We've seen a company that labeled its change initiative as "successful" because employee motivation questionnaires indicated that satisfaction had increased from 76.6 to 77.4 percent over one year. The inspiring, visionary approach may make people passionate for change but leave them without concrete objectives. In reconciling corporate cultures, inspiring visions/philosophies are used to create the energy needed to reach concrete, measurable objectives.

Top-down driven change versus bottom-up initiated change

In top-down driven change, it is clear who is in control and makes decisions. However in its extreme this leads to "change hero leaders" who "roll out" planned change programs and soon run out of energy when they discover that they have failed to gain the commitment of organizational members. Participative change processes, involving people at all levels, often end up in compromises because conflicts are avoided. Reconciling corporate cultures involve all stakeholder groups in agreeing on the direction of change and the reasons for moving in that direction, handle conflict openly, and entrust responsibilities to change agents at all levels, so that through getting people truly involved, commitment is truly gained.

Change from within versus change driven by external events

Change from within to improve competencies, internal business processes, and innovative capability may in its extreme form lead to an inward-looking mentality and the "Not Invented Here" syndrome. Change driven by external events helps in adapting to changing customer demands and developments in markets and technology, but may give people in the organization the feeling that they are on a rudderless ship. In reconciling corporate cultures, change takes place by cross-fertilization of developments inside and outside the company and by internalizing external innovation.

Change to increase short-term shareholder value versus change to improve long-term, sustainable stakeholder value

Change initiatives focused on maximizing shareholder value as quickly as possible often lead to superficial change because only the outer levels of corporate culture (the practices) are addressed. Change initiatives focused on sustainable stakeholder value are often limited to hollow statements about environmental responsibility, integrity, and corporate citizenship, without a real effort to challenge basic assumptions. In reconciling corporate cultures, the willingness and ability to listen to those stakeholders who do challenge basic assumptions results in profound change through new definitions of performance, profitability, and shareholder value, which include broader social and environmental impacts of the company's operations.

Change by great leaps versus incremental change/continuous improvement (Kaizen)

Great leaps and breakthrough events may be necessary to accelerate change but are at risk of disrupting the whole organization. Incremental change has proven its value as "continuous improvement" or "Kaizen," but may not be radical enough in current business environments. In reconciling corporate cultures, change and continuity are connected as in "continuity through renewal" – through showing people that change is necessary to preserve what is most valuable to them, such as innovative capability, close customer contact, informality, or open communication. By doing this breakthrough change becomes more acceptable.

We have argued in this book that the existing corporate culture itself determines what kind of corporate culture change will be accepted. Reconciling corporate cultures continuously check to see if they still fit the competitive environment. They create space for continuous dialogue, accept complexity, and foster a mindset aimed at openly handling conflicts by connecting opposites instead of by breaking resistance, thereby ensuring that all organizational members develop the skills and attitudes to deal with ongoing change. In reconciling corporate cultures, change is a way of life, a self-sustaining spiral.

Bibliography

Abraham, M., Fisher, T., and Crawford, J. (1997) "Quality Culture and the Management of Organization Change," *International Journal of Quality and Reliability Management*, June, 14(6–7), 616.

Abrahamson, E. (2000) "Change Without Pain," *Harvard Business Review*, 78, July/August, 75–79.

Anders, G. (2003) *Perfect Enough: Carly Fiorina and the Reinvention of Hewlett-Packard*. New York: Portfolio

Asser, M. and Hampden-Turner, C. (2001) "The Internet as an Environment for Business Ecosystems," in F. Trompenaars and C. Hampden-Turner, *21 Leaders for the 21st Century*. Oxford: Capstone, pp. 215–232

Bennett, J. (1998) "Constrained Change, Unconstrained Results," *Strategy Management Competition*, Third Quarter 1998 (http://www.strategy-business.com/strategy/98303/page1.html).

Bennis, W. and O'Toole, J. (2000) "Don't Hire the Wrong CEO," *Harvard Business Review*, 78, May/June, 171–176.

Bernstein, A. and Hof, R. (2000) "A Union for Amazon," *Business Week*, 4 December, 86–88.

Bohannan, P. (1995) *How Culture Works*. New York: Free Press.

Booker, K. (2001) "The Chairman of the Board Looks Back," *Fortune*, 28 May.

Boston, W. and Kempe, F. (2001) "For Siemens CEO, the Goal is Game, Set and Match," *Wall Street Journal*, 2 February.

Bratton, J. (1992) *Japanization at Work*. Basingstoke: Macmillan Press.

Burrows, P. (2003) *Backfire*. New York: John Wiley.

Business Week (1984) "Oops!" 5 November.

Business Week (1999) "Gurus Who Failed their Own Course," 8 November.

Business Week (2002) "He's Putting Siemens on the American Map," 4 February.

Business Week (2003) "Was the Merger a Mistake?" 29 September.

Cameron, S.K. and Quinn, R.E. (1999) *Diagnosing and Changing Organizational Culture*. Reading, MA: Addison-Wesley.

Campbell, N. and Burton, F. (1994) *Japanese Multinationals: Strategies and Management in the Global Kaisha*. London: Routledge

Caudron, S. (2003) "Don't Mess With Carly," *Workforce*, July, 15

Chin, R. and Benne, K.D. (1969) "General Strategies for Effecting Changes in Human Systems," in W.G. Bennis, K.D. Benne, and R. Chin (eds), *The Planning of Change*. New York: Holt, Rinehart and Winston, pp. 32–59.

Collins, J. (2001) *Good to Great*. New York: Random House.

Collins, J. and Porras, J.I. (1994) *Built to Last*. London: Century.

Colvin, G. and Huey, J. (1999) "The Jack and Herb Show," *Fortune*, 11 January.

Deal, T.E. and Kennedy, A.A. (1982) *Corporate Cultures: The Rites and Rituals of Corporate Life*. Reading, MA: Addison-Wesley.

Deal, T.E. and Kennedy, A.A. (1999) *The New Corporate Cultures*. Cambridge, MA: Perseus.

de Geus, A.P. (1997) *The Living Company*. London: Nicholas Brealey.

Dell, M. (1999) *Direct from Dell: Strategies that Revolutionized an Industry*. New York: Harper Business.

Economist (1994) "The Discreet Charm of the Multicultural Multinational," 30 July.

Economist (2000) "The DaimlerChrysler Emulsion," 29 July.

Economist (2003) "A European Giant Stirs," 13 February.

Ewing, J. (2000) "Siemens Climbs Back," *Business Week*, 5 June, 48–52.

Fekete, S. (2003) *Companies are People Too*. New York: John Wiley

Fiorina, C. (2001) "The Business of Change," speech at TIECON 2001, Santa Clara, CA, 23 June 2001 (www.hp.com).

Fox, L. (2003) *Enron: The Rise and Fall*. Hoboken: John Wiley.

Freiberg, K. and Freiberg, J. (1996) *Nuts! Southwest Airlines' Crazy Recipe for Business and Personal Success*. Austin, TX: Bard Press.

Gerstner, L. (2002) *Who Says Elephants Can't Dance?* New York, HarperCollins

Gittell, J.H. (2002) *The Southwest Airlines Way: Using the Power of Relationships to Achieve High Performance*. NewYork: McGraw-Hill

Goffee, R. and Jones, G. (1996). "What Holds the Modern Company Together?" *Harvard Business Review*, 74, November/December, 133–148.

Grove, A. (1996). *Only the Paranoid Survive*. New York: Currency-Doubleday

Harrison, D. (1999) "Barriers to Change," *HR Focus*, 76(7), 9.

Hayashi, S. (1988) *Culture and Management in Japan*. Tokyo: University of Tokyo Press.

Hofstede, G. (1991) *Cultures and Organizations: Software of the Mind*. New York: McGraw-Hill.

Hofstede, G. (2001) *Culture's Consequences*, 2nd edn. Thousand Oaks, CA: Sage.

Hofstede, G., Neuijen, B., Ohayv, D. and Sanders, G. (1990) "Measuring Organizational Cultures: A Qualitative and Quantitiative Analysis across Twenty Cases," *Administrative Science Quarterly*, 35, 286–316.

James, G. (1998) *Success Secrets from Silicon Valley*. New York: Times Business

Johansson, J. and Nonaka, I. (1996) *Relentless: The Japanese Way of Marketing*. New York: Harper Business.

Kearney, A.T. (2000) "Change Management," *The Economist* (US), 15 July, 356(8179), 61.

Kelleher, H. (1999) "Culture is Your Number One Priority," in T.J. Neff and J.C. Citrin (eds), *Lessons from the Top*. New York: Doubleday, pp. 187–92.

Kotter, J.P. and Heskett, J.L. (1992) *Corporate Culture and Performance*. New York: The Free Press.

Lee, C.M., Miller, W., Hancock, M.G., and Rowen, H.S. (2000) *The Silicon Valley Edge: A Habitat for Innovation and Entrepreneurship*. Stanford, CA: Stanford University Press

Lewis, M. (2000) *The New, New Thing: A Silicon Valley Story*. New York: W.W. Norton.

3M Company. (2002). *A Century of Innovation*. St Paul: 3M Company (www.3M.com).

Malmsten, E., Portanger, E., and Drazin, C. (2002) *Boohoo: A Dot-Com Story from Concept to Catastrophe*. London: Arrow.

March, R. (1992) *Working for a Japanese Company*. Tokyo: Kodansha

McLean, B. and Elkind, P. (2003) *Smartest Guys in the Room: The Amazing Rise and Scandalous Fall of Enron*. New York: Portfolio

McShane, S. and Von Glinow, M.A. (2003) *Organizational Behaviour*, 2nd edn. New York: McGraw-Hill

Morgan, J.C. and Morgan, J.J. (1991) *Cracking the Japanese Market*. New York: The Free Press.

Morita, A. (1986) *Made in Japan*. New York: E.P. Dutton.

Nathan, J. (1999) *Sony*. Boston, MA: Houghton Mifflin Company.

Neuhauser, P., Bender, R., and Stromberg, K. (2000) *Culture.com: Building Corporate Culture in the Connected Workplace*. New York: John Wiley

Newsweek (2002) Interview with Jim Morgan, 29 April, p. 54.

Nonaka, I. and Takeuchi, H. (1995) *The Knowledge-Creating Company*. New York: Oxford University Press.

NRC Handelsblad (2002) "Smits verliest van bankbaronnen," 3 September.

Park, A. and Burrows, P. (2003) "What You Don't Know About Dell," *Business Week*, 3 November, 46–54.

Pascale, R.T. and Athos, A.G. (1981) *The Art of Japanese Management*. New York: Simon and Schuster.

Peters, T.J. and Waterman, R.H. (1982) *In Search of Excellence*. New York: Harper and Row.

Prud'homme, P. (2001) "Global Brand, Local Touch," in F. Trompenaars and C. Hampden-Turner, *21 Leaders for the 21st Century*. Oxford: Capstone, pp. 233–252.

Prud'homme, P. and Schrijen, N. (2002). "Fortis: How flexible solutions resulted in a solid Dutch-Belgian partnership," in Spencer Stuart Executive Search Consultants and Trompenaars Hampden-Turner, *Leading Cross-Border Mergers*. Amsterdam: Spencer Stuart, pp. 89–112.

Prud'homme, P. and Trompenaars, F. (2001). "Private Enterprise, Public Service," in F. Trompenaars and C. Hampden-Turner, *21 Leaders for the 21st Century*. Oxford: Capstone, pp. 153–172.

Sashkin, M., and Egermeier, J. (1992) "Models and Processes for Change," *Insight*, Winter, 24–29.

Saunders, R. (2001) *Business the Amazon.com Way*. London: Capstone

Saxenian, A.L. (1994) *Regional Advantage: Culture and Competition in Silicon Valley and Route 128*. Cambridge, MA: Harvard University Press.

Slater, R. (1993) *The New GE: How Jack Welch Revived an American Institution*. Homewood, IL: Business One Irwin.

Schein, E. H. (1985) *Organizational Culture and Leadership*. San Francisco, CA: Jossey-Bass.

Schultz, H. (1999) "Sharing Success, Starbucks," in T.J. Neff and J.C. Citrin (eds), *Lessons from the Top*. New York: Doubleday, pp. 259–264.

Schultz, H. (1997) *Pour Your Heart Into It: How Starbucks Built a Company One Cup at a Time*. Westport, CN: Hyperion Press.

Shih, S. (1996) *Me-Too Is Not My Style*. Taipei: Acer Foundation.

Spector, W. (2000) *Amazon.com: Get Big Fast*. New York: Random House

Spyckerelle, J. and Hampden-Turner, C. (2001) "Leading through Transformation," in F. Trompenaars, and C. Hampden-Turner, *21 Leaders for the 21st Century*. Oxford: Capstone.

Squires, S.E., Smith, C., McDougall, L., and Yeack, W.E. (2003) *Inside Arthur Andersen: Shifting Values, Unexpected Consequences*. London: Financial Times Prentice Hall

Steinbeck, J. (1962) *Travels with Charley: In Search of America*. New York: Viking Press.

Steinbock, D. (2001) *The Nokia Revolution: The Story of an Extraordinary Company that Transformed an Industry*. New York: AMACOM.

Toffler, B.E. and Reingold, J. (2003) *Final Accounting: Ambition, Greed, and the Fall of Arthur Andersen*. New York: Broadway Books.

Torekull, B. (1998). *Leading by Design: The IKEA Story*. New York: Harper-Business.

Trice, H. M. and Beyer, J. M. (1984) "Studying Organizational Culture Through Rites and Rituals," *Academy of Management Review*, 9, 653–669.

Trompenaars, F. and Hampden-Turner, C. (1997). *Riding the Waves of Culture*. London: Nicholas Brealey.

Trompenaars, F. and Hampden-Turner, C. (2003) *Managing People Across Cultures*. London: Capstone.

Trompenaars, F., Prud'homme, P., Park, J.H. and Hampden-Turner, C. (2001). "Pioneering the New Organization," in F. Trompenaars and C. Hampden-Turner, *21 Leaders for the 21st Century*. Oxford: Capstone, pp. 193–214.

Trompenaars, F. and Woolliams, P. (2003) *Business Across Cultures*. London: Capstone.

Vlasic, B. and Stertz, B.A. (2000). *Taken for a Ride: How Daimler-Benz Drove off With Chrysler*. New York: Harper Collins.

Von Pierer, H. and Van Oetinger, B. (2001) *A Passion for Ideas: How Innovators Create the New and Shape Our World*. West Lafayette, IN: Purdue University Press.

Watkins, S. and Swartz, M. (2003) *Power Failure: The Inside Story of the Collapse of Enron*. New York: Doubleday.

Weick, K.E. and Sutcliffe, K.E. (2003) "Hospitals as Cultures of Entrapment," *California Management Review*, 45(2), 73–83.

Welch, J. (2001) *Straight from the Gut*. New York: Warner Books.

Index

Trompenaars Hampden-Turner

Culture for Business

Trompenaars Hampden-Turner provides consulting, training, coaching, and (un)learning services to help leaders and professionals manage and solve their business and culture dilemmas. Our clients are primarily Global Fortune 500 companies. We are based in Amsterdam, the Netherlands and Boston, USA. In addition, we have a network of associates throughout the world.

We particularly focus on cross-cultural consulting services around:

- mergers and acquisitions integration
- globalization
- corporate vision and values.

We take pride in using the client's own language and discourse, although we make subtle changes to its underlying structure to render it more coherent. Topics may include diversity, communication, learning, training, teamwork, culture, coaching, knowledge management, leadership development, integrity, and balanced scorecards. For us these are all parts of a system. We also aim to introduce our clients to a paradoxical logic of human and organizational development. We aim for minimalist interventions yielding maximum results.

Introduction to our offerings

We work with all business implications of culture. These may be part of an organization's globalization process, external growth and integration strategies, corporate identity and corporate communications, international change management, or the worldwide "roll-out" of building cross-cultural competencies.

We work with organizations through a highly customized and integrated approach including:

Consulting on culture-for-business management

- Conduct cross-cultural due diligence
- Facilitate your vision and value to strengthen your corporate identity
- Surface cultural challenges and dilemmas which may be creating obstacles
- Systematically reconcile cultural differences in order to maximize the business value of cultural diversity
- Assist in creating a business climate of mutual respect and trust in order to link people from different cultures in productive and positive ways.

Global leadership development

- Create top-of-mind recognition of and respect for cross-cultural issues
- Develop culture-for-business competencies into competitive advantage
- Help leaders solve critical culture-for-business dilemmas
- Ascertain awareness of and respect for cross-cultural diversity
- Develop the ability to leverage global diversity.

Executive coaching

- Cross-cultural executive coaching helps leaders and managers with wider perspectives, cultural sensitivity, and the ability to work with diversity in a productive and innovative way to achieve organizational goals.

- Cross-cultural coaching helps the individual or team assess its own strengths and challenges. It assists with positive changes in behavior and perception. It also helps individual integration without sacrificing diversity and integrity within the organization.

Employee training and (un)learning

- Raise awareness of how culture-for-business competencies can help improve the bottom line
- Build awareness and respect for cross-culture and diversity issues
- Provide support in "unlearning" negative cultural attitudes and stereotypes
- Develop the ability to value and work with diversity.

Amsterdam Office:

A.J. Ernststraat 595D
1082 LD Amsterdam
The Netherlands
Tel: +31 20 301 6666
Fax: +31 20 301 6555
Email: info@thtconsulting.com

USA Office:

14 Arrow Street, Suite 10
Cambridge, MA 02138-5106
USA
Tel: +1 617 876 5025
Fax: +1 617 876 5026

tions, international change management, or the worldwide "roll-out" of building cross-cultural competencies.

We work with organizations through a highly customized and integrated approach including:

Consulting on culture-for-business management

- Conduct cross-cultural due diligence
- Facilitate your vision and value to strengthen your corporate identity
- Surface cultural challenges and dilemmas which may be creating obstacles
- Systematically reconcile cultural differences in order to maximize the business value of cultural diversity
- Assist in creating a business climate of mutual respect and trust in order to link people from different cultures in productive and positive ways.

Global leadership development

- Create top-of-mind recognition of and respect for cross-cultural issues
- Develop culture-for-business competencies into competitive advantage
- Help leaders solve critical culture-for-business dilemmas
- Ascertain awareness of and respect for cross-cultural diversity
- Develop the ability to leverage global diversity.

Executive coaching

- Cross-cultural executive coaching helps leaders and managers with wider perspectives, cultural sensitivity, and the ability to work with diversity in a productive and innovative way to achieve organizational goals.

- Cross-cultural coaching helps the individual or team assess its own strengths and challenges. It assists with positive changes in behavior and perception. It also helps individual integration without sacrificing diversity and integrity within the organization.

Employee training and (un)learning

- Raise awareness of how culture-for-business competencies can help improve the bottom line
- Build awareness and respect for cross-culture and diversity issues
- Provide support in "unlearning" negative cultural attitudes and stereotypes
- Develop the ability to value and work with diversity.

Amsterdam Office:

A.J. Ernststraat 595D
1082 LD Amsterdam
The Netherlands
Tel: +31 20 301 6666
Fax: +31 20 301 6555
Email: info@thtconsulting.com

USA Office:

14 Arrow Street, Suite 10
Cambridge, MA 02138-5106
USA
Tel: +1 617 876 5025
Fax: +1 617 876 5026

YEOVIL COLLEGE
LIBRARY